Volleyball was founded by: William C. Morgan in 1895 at Holyoke Mass. at a YMCA.

Volleyball

second edition

Allen E. Scates

Physical Education Specialist, Beverly Hills School District
Head Volleyball Coach, University of California, Los Angeles
NCAA Champions 1970, 1971, 1972, 1974, 1975
Head Coach of U.S.A. Mens Team
Head Pan-American and Olympic Coach

Jane Ward

Cabrillo College, Aptos, California
Former Captain, U.S. Olympic Team
Head Coach, California State University at San Jose
Head Pan-American Coach

ALLYN AND BACON, INC.
BOSTON · LONDON · SYDNEY · TORONTO

Copyright © 1975, 1969 by Allyn and Bacon, Inc.,
470 Atlantic Avenue, Boston, Massachusetts 02210.

All rights reserved. Printed in the United States of America. No part of the material protected by this copyright notice may be reproduced or utilized in any form or by any means, electronic or mechanical, including photocopying, recording, or by any information storage or retrieval system, without written permission from the copyright owner.

Library of Congress Cataloging in Publication Data

Scates, Allen E
  Volleyball.

  Includes bibliographical references.
  1. Volleyball. I. Ward, Jane, joint author.
GV1017.V6S27   1975   796.32'5   75—6583

ISBN 0—205—04817—X

Fifth printing . . . February, 1978

Contents

Foreword v

Preface vii

1 Volleyball—A Team Sport for All Ages and Abilities 1
2 Essential Skills for Power Volleyball 7
3 Volleyball Rules 35
4 Basic Offensive and Defensive Strategies 41
5 Advanced Skills for Power Players 58
6 Preparation for Power Volleyball Competition 78
7 Where to Play 87
8 Further Study Materials 90

Foreword

Sports, exercise, and other forms of physical activity are important facets of our culture. Recognizing this fact, Allyn and Bacon in 1969 started to publish a unique and distinctive series of books on the basic concepts and skills of a number of physical activities. As a result of the popularity and usefulness of these publications, the original books have gone into second editions and the number of books in the series has been expanded. These books represent a high point in curriculum design; reading them is like having a lesson plan for teaching or learning the activities.

The conceptual approach has been used in the development of these books. This approach starts with the identification of *key concepts* around which the activity is structured. These statements and the subconcepts that support them serve as the basis for organizing and relating the facts and skills of the activity into a meaningful whole. The learner is guided in developing these cognitive and motor concepts through a series of *learning experiences*. These experiences are designed to involve the learner in the learning process, both intellectually and physically. Each experience leads the learner to develop specific behaviors. Where applicable, at the end of each key concept a list of these behaviors *(outcomes)* is provided to enable the student to determine if he or she is learning. If he can demonstrate that he has achieved these outcomes, he can be confident that he has conceptualized the material and should be able to perform the activity with some degree of proficiency. The emphasis is upon skill development.

Although these books are designed primarily to be used for beginning instructional classes, sections have been included for intermediate and advanced classes. Their unique structure and clear presentation enable a student to learn the activity even without the direction of a teacher if necessary.

The authors have been selected on a national scale. All have excellent backgrounds as performers and teachers. The combination of these high calibre teachers and the conceptual organization of the material has produced a series of books that will be of great value in improving instruction in physical education, particularly in high school and college classes.

Alyce Cheska
University of Illinois

Raymond A. Snyder
University of California, Los Angeles

Preface

This is a complete and concise volleyball experience developed by two of the nation's finest coaches. The first part of the book contains comprehensive and accurate descriptions of fundamentals and strategy written for the player who is interested in the sport but has little or no volleyball background. Consequently only the basic skills and concepts are included, stated in terms designed to be simple, clear and complete to the younger player and beginner. Illustrations of All American, Pan American and Olympic players demonstrate the basic skills to be experienced by the reader.

Also included in the book is a detailed explanation of the advanced skills and concepts of play necessary for maximum performance: what to look for, how to use plays, what sort of defense to use, and variations in the attack.

1

Volleyball – A Team Sport for All Ages and Abilities

CONCEPT: The universal game of volleyball can be adapted to the needs and ability of any participant.

Volleyball is a popular participant sport for all ages and levels of ability. It does not require expensive or elaborate equipment and facilities. The modification of the rules at the elementary level, lenient interpretation at the junior and senior high school and recreational league levels, and strict observance of the technical rules at the highly competitive level enable the game to be adapted to participants of all abilities, thus making it one of the most popular participation sports in the United States today.

People compete in volleyball for many different reasons. When volleyball was first developed in the United States, it was devised as a nonstrenuous game requiring little or no skill, for the purpose of fun and relaxation. It is still played by many with these same requirements of ability and purpose. It is also an excellent social game, the rules having been adapted to coeducational play. It is not only a popular family and group recreational game, but it offers a challenge for the highly skilled player in the form of a game called "doubles," or two on a side. Volleyball appeals to people of all ages at different levels of skill, and with various objectives in mind. The housewife in the recreational league and the businessman at the YMCA play for exercise, fun, and relaxation; heterogeneous and homogeneous social groups play for activity and entertainment. On the other hand, the highly skilled athlete who competes at the intercollegiate or national level plays not only for the physical activity and social outcomes, but also for the high degree of competition volleyball affords.

Volleyball has grown from a sport requiring little ability to a highly competitive game where speed, strength, endurance and coordination are of the utmost importance. The reason that "power" volleyball has been so slow in developing in this country is that there has been a lack of qualified people to teach the basic skills and correct interpretation of the rules so essential for performance.

1. The rules and strategy of volleyball are basically the same for men and women.

The only difference is the height of the net. The game is played on a court divided into two equal parts by a center line and net, which is 7'4¼" high for women and 8' high for men.

The teams line up on the court, with three front row and three back row players, before the ball is served. The team receiving the *serve* has three hits with which to get the ball back over the net. There is usually a definite pattern in playing the ball; that is, the first ball over the net is passed to a player who is called a *setter*. The setter in turn "sets" the ball high in the air, close to the net, for the *spiker;* this player runs in, jumps into the air and tries to spike the ball down into the opponents' court so that it cannot be returned. With the offensive team making use of their three hits to spike the ball, the opponents must form a block in front of the spiker in an attempt to prevent the ball from hitting the floor. With the advent of the spike and the attempt to block by the defensive team, there arise other offensive and defensive individual and team techniques that must be developed to complement the game. The higher the degree of individual ability, the more the advanced skills and techniques of the game need to be mastered.

After the ball is served, it becomes the job of the serving team to prevent the ball from being returned over the net so that a point can be scored, for it is only the serving team which can score points. The receiving team tries to return the ball and force it to become *dead* in the server's court, so as to create a "side-out" and an exchange of service. Often the ball continues in play by crossing the net several times, as a result of the defensive team blocking or digging the spike—this is called a *rally.* When the receiving team gains the ball to serve, the team must rotate in a clockwise motion, with the right back player going behind the baseline to serve the ball.

A game is won by the team that has scored the most points and is at least two points ahead: a) when one team has scored 15 points, or b) the first time the ball becomes dead after eight minutes of play, whichever occurs first. If the leading team does not have a two-point advantage, unlimited overtime shall be played. A team winning two games wins the match.

2. Volleyball is one of the leading participant sports in Europe and Asia, and is gaining popularity in the United States since its inclusion in the Olympics in 1964.

With the publicity the Japanese women brought to the game of volleyball through their intensified training program and the winning of the gold medal in the 1964 Olympic Games, volleyball in this country and the

Southern Hemisphere has progressed by leaps and bounds. The Japanese Nichibo Women's team added a new phase to volleyball—the perfection of the greatest defenses ever seen in the game. They included tumbling in their fundamental skills, they dove on the floor to save all kinds of hard hit spikes, digging the ball into the air with great control, rolling over and landing on their feet ready for the next play. Their great speed and conditioning, and their ability to go on the floor without the fear of injury made their defense just about impenetrable.

Learning Experience

Look up the records of the men's and women's volleyball standings in the World Games and Olympics since 1964. Which area of the world had the most entries? Which area consistently finished in the top five positions?

The game of volleyball in Europe and Asia ranks as one of the most popular participant and spectator sports. Matches between the top national teams in the Iron Curtain countries have been known to attract as many as 50,000 spectators.

The excellent calibre of play in these countries was outstanding until the Japanese demonstrated even more spectacular volleyball, particularly from a defensive point of view.

The development of the international offense by both European and Asian countries was a refinement and a strong improvement over our American game. Here in the United States, one of the three players in the front row was a "set up" player, which limited our attack with the remaining two front row spikers. The international system, on the other hand, by running the "set up" player in from the back row, provided the team with three offensive front row spikers. This pattern made it more difficult for the defensive team to provide an adequate block against the multiple offense.

Volleyball in the Southern Hemisphere has also been a very popular sport, but has lacked the competent coaching so necessary to produce teams of top international calibre. Teams are continually upgrading their programs by importing coaches from Asian and European countries to improve the techniques necessary for international competition.

After seeing the great success the Japanese had in this type of game, many teams adopted their defensive techniques, particularly those in the United States. With the additional adoption of the international offensive system and the Japanese defensive system, the United States went to work to develop their top players in these various techniques. The continued use of these techniques and strenuous conditioning procedures brought about a major upset in the first match of the 1968 Olympics, where the

United States men defeated the Russians for the first time. The National Collegiate Athletic Association, the National Association of Intercollegiate Athletics, the National Junior College Athletic Association, the United States Volleyball Association and the Association of Intercollegiate Athletics for Women hold national championships. This has hastened the development of the sport at the junior and senior high school levels.

3. Power volleyball, played on a highly competitive level, demands a well-coordinated athlete with an even temperament and the ability to develop strength and endurance.

The athlete interested in this sport at the power level should be willing to devote a great deal of time to it. The volleyball season in the United States begins in the Fall and culminates with national tournaments in May. International World University Games, Pan American Games and Olympic Games competition come at various times, some within the seasonal span, and some not. In Southern California and Hawaii, where volleyball is played on the beach, it is a year-round sport.

The development of a player's strength and endurance is possible, but a player must have natural coordination. The conditioning program for the top volleyball player is grueling and time consuming. A player must, therefore, be dedicated enough to work on his own, and be willing to submit himself to some physical punishment. To condition an athlete to play at maximum efficiency takes months of intensive training. A player must be able to spike in three positions across the net, and to block in three positions; then rotate to the back court, where for three positions he must move quickly on every offensive and defensive play, must dive to the floor again and again and come up quickly for the next play.

Attaining this kind of physical condition and skill is a difficult task. The volleyball athlete should run stairs and do sit-ups and push-ups for general conditioning. Toe raises and squats with weights strengthen the legs and give them greater endurance. Hours must be spent in going to the floor to retrieve balls, so that response becomes automatic. These drills are necessary in order to prepare the individual for maximum performance during an entire match; men's intercollegiate and all international matches which go to five games can last up to three hours. A recent NCAA Championship Match lasted three hours and fifteen minutes.

Individual work must be combined with team drills to complete the practice schedule. Considerable time must be spent on teamwork, so that the entire squad performs as a cohesive unit. Volleyball is truly a *team* sport.

Time involved for practice usually depends on the team for which one plays. Most teams that play in the United States Volleyball Association tournaments practice twice a week throughout the season, with monthly tournaments scheduled. They may practice three to six times a week, for three weeks or a month prior to a national tournament. Many varsity college women's volleyball programs are conducted during the fall. Better teams practice every day school is in session. After their championships in December, many of the women join an "open" team, which competes in United States Volleyball Association tournaments. Laural Brassey became the first woman to compete on a men's intercollegiate volleyball team when she played for San Diego State University during the 1974 season. Men's intercollegiate programs begin in the winter with daily practice; the championship events are held in late April or early May. Practice sessions for Pan American and Olympic team members usually run from four to six weeks, and from six to seven hours a day. U.S. team members often tour Europe for a month or more during the summer to compete against top international teams.

Physical qualifications are not all that is necessary to qualify a player for top-level competition. Psychological temperament is also an important factor. A player cannot be highly temperamental, since fits of anger or other anxieties may cause the quality of performance to fall below par. Neither can the player be one who, after a mistake or two, completely loses composure and fails to meet the requirements of stress put on him. A player cannot be an individual on the court. He cannot try to play every ball or wait for every set. He must always act in relation to the overall team effort.

The volleyball player must be able to recover from individual mistakes, must maintain an even temperament, must perform on the court for the benefit of the team as a whole, and must be able to sustain a competitive drive for a long period of time.

Learning Experience

What is your purpose in learning to play volleyball? Are you willing to develop the skill and physical condition to participate in high level competition, or are you satisfied with recreational play? What factors influenced your decision?

OUTCOMES

1. State why volleyball is a very popular sport in the United States.
2. List various reasons why different types of people play volleyball.

3. Explain why "power" volleyball has been so slow to develop in the United States.
4. Explain the basic play pattern utilizing three hits.
5. How does a team score points, and what is involved in a team's effort to get a point?
6. Diagram the starting position of players and illustrate how they rotate when they gain the serve.
7. What constitutes a game and a match?
8. What basic techniques have been adopted by the U.S. teams to improve their calibre of team play?
9. How has the acceptance of volleyball as an NCAA and AIAW sport helped the development of the game?
10. What physical attributes are necessary to become a top-level player?
11. What kind of a conditioning program is necessary to train a volleyball athlete?
12. What kind of psychological temperament is necessary in a good player?

2

Essential Skills for Power Volleyball

CONCEPT: The skills of serving, passing, setting, spiking, digging and blocking are necessary for successful participation in power volleyball.

As was stated earlier, the skills of volleyball can be adapted to all ages and abilities. The beginning skills necessary for participation in the game should be learned, and as these abilities and individual goals increase, so should the degree of difficulty of the skills.

1. The ball is put into play by a serve.

Since the serve is necessary for a team to score points, one must use a serve that can be depended upon within the server's capabilities. If the serve cannot be controlled and accurately placed, the offensive advantage is immediately lost. There are three basic serves:

a) The *underhand serve*, the easiest one to execute and control.
b) The *overhand "floater"* serve, having no spin, and moving in an erratic path as it approaches the receiver; used by the overwhelming majority of advanced men and women players.
c) The *overhand spin serve*, going fast and dropping quickly; difficult to receive, and also more difficult to master.

1a. The underhand serve is the easiest to execute and control. It requires very little strength, in contrast to the overhand serve. It is not a strong offensive weapon and, therefore, not much of a threat to opponents unless some "floating" action can be imparted.

The server stands behind the legal area of the baseline, squarely facing the net with the left foot forward (for a right-handed person) and the knees slightly bent (Fig. 2.1). The ball is held in the palm of the left hand, directly in line with the right foot. The right arm is swung directly back and straight forward. The ball is contacted with the heel of the hand, if the hand is open, or the heel of the hand and a portion of the fingers, if the hand is closed. The head remains down and the eyes are directly on the ball. At the point of contact the weight shifts from the right to left foot, and the arm follows-through in the direction of intended flight of the ball.

The point of contact on the ball is determined by the direction of flight the server wishes the ball to travel. If the ball is to go straight ahead, it must be struck in the center, just below the midsection. If the ball is to travel to the left of the server, it must be struck just below the midsection in the lower right quarter. If the ball is to travel to the right of the server, it must be struck in the lower left quarter.

It is important that the position of the body and the ball and the direction of the arm swing remain the same for all serves. Otherwise, the intended direction of the serve might be "given away" to the opponents before the ball is struck. For the beginner, it is easier to learn to contact the ball only at the center, below the midsection, and follow through in a straight line. In order to change the direction of the serve, the beginner should merely turn his body position so that his feet point in the direction of the intended flight of the ball.

Common errors and corrections in the underhand serve are: 1) *Hitting the ball into the net.* This may be due to a) the server taking his eyes off the ball and looking up before contact, thus causing his upper body to rise, changing the plane or arc of the arm swing, forcing him to contact the ball higher than the midsection, or b) dropping the ball out of the hand before contact. 2) *Hitting the ball high into the air.* This is caused by contacting the ball too far below the midsection. The ball may be held too high in the left hand, causing the fist to strike the bottom of the ball with a normal arm swing, or the server may be allowing the shoulder of his serving arm to dip below the level of the left shoulder. The server must be aware of how he is holding the ball, so that as his arm swings naturally, the hand will contact the ball at the desired area. 3) *Hitting the ball out of the court, long, or to the right or left.* a) This, too, may be caused by contact at the improper area. The arm may be swinging too far across the

Figure 2.1. Underhand Serve

body, causing the ball to go left; or the arm may be swinging too far away from the body, causing the ball to go right. Holding the ball too near the center of the body, or too far outside the right foot, may also cause the ball to go left or right. b) Too fast or too powerful an arm swing will cause the ball to go long out of the court. The heel of the hand offers a "springing" action to the ball, similar to a baseball hitting a bat; therefore, not too much force is required to get the ball over the net.

Learning Experience: Underhand Serve, Stance

Stand behind the baseline, face the net squarely, feet in a stride position, left ahead of the right. Contact the ball in the center just below the midsection, with a straight back swing and follow-through of the arm. Serve ten times. Does the ball go in the same direction each time?

Now stand facing the left side of the net and contact the ball in the same spot. Does the ball go to the right side of your opponents' court? Repeat ten times, facing the right front of the net.

Do you get accurate placement of the serve, with the same arm swing and point of contact, merely by changing the direction your body faces?

Learning Experience: Underhand Serve, Contacting the Ball

Stand behind the baseline, face the net squarely, left foot forward, right back. Contact the ball on the right quarter, just below the midsection, and follow through to the left of intended flight. Does the ball travel to your left, landing in the opponents' right court?

Using the same stance, swing your arm and contact the ball on the left quarter just below the midsection, and follow through in the direction of intended flight. Does the ball travel to your right, landing in the opponents' left court?

1b. The overhand "floater" serve, having no spin, moves in an erratic path as it approaches the receiver and is difficult to pass. The first pass should be made so there is no loud sound or prolonged contact with the ball. To achieve this, the receiver's body should be in line with the oncoming ball. A floater or "moving" ball makes it difficult for the receiver to achieve this. The floater has the tendency to make the ball drop, rise, or move right or left as it approaches the receiver.

To achieve the floater serve, the ball is held in the left hand (for a right-handed player), approximately chest high, directly in line with the right foot. The ball is usually tossed two or three feet in the air. As the ball drops in front of and above the right shoulder, the arm should quickly extend from a cocked position and the ball should be contacted just one or two inches below the center with the heel of the hand. Some players prefer an alternate method. They hold the ball in the left hand (for a right-handed server), approximately one to two feet above the right shoulder, directly in line with the right foot. As the arm swings quickly from a cocked position, the ball is lowered in the hand to a position just above the right shoulder. The ball is contacted almost directly out of the left hand, one or two inches below the midsection with the heel of the hand. Regardless of which method is used there is a weight shift from the back to the front foot during contact. Many players prefer to take a short step forward with their front feet just prior to contact. There is little follow-through with the hand or arm on this serve. The ball is jabbed or punched with only a momentary point of contact, and the arm action stops almost immediately. This quick action on the ball just below the center causes it to take off over the net with a "wiggle" type of motion, dropping, rising, or just moving from side to side, similar to the knuckleball in baseball.

A common error and correction in the floater serve is: *No "action" on the ball.* This is caused by too much follow-through with the arm and hand or too much contact area on the ball. You must work on a quick jabbing action and be sure to hit below the center. You must also get force into your jab by keeping your wrist stiff and hitting directly with the heel of your hand.

Learning Experience: Floater Serve

Assume the correct stance behind the baseline. Serve the ball over the net to a partner. Can your partner see any "wiggle" in the flight of the ball? Can you?

After you can get the ball to float, place a rope approximately 6 feet above the height of the net. Try to serve the ball under the rope, deep to the back line, landing within a line 3 feet from and parallel to the end line. Does it help to stand close to, or away from the service line to achieve this serve?

1c. The overhand spin serve results in a fast dropping action, which gives the opposition less time to react. It is not as easily controlled by the server as the floater serve, and for that reason is rarely used. Due to the spinning action of this serve, the flight of the ball is very predictable, in comparison to the wobbly flight of the floater serve.

To learn the overhand spin serve, a right-handed individual starts behind the baseline, facing the net, left foot in front. The ball is tossed softly two to four feet above the head and slightly in front of the right shoulder. The right arm is brought back so the hand is just behind the head and held open, the shoulders rotate so the left shoulder faces the net, and the

ESSENTIAL SKILLS FOR POWER VOLLEYBALL

Photographs courtesy of Stan Abraham

Figure 2.2. Overhand Serve

weight is on the back foot. The arm straightens and extends so that the ball is contacted on its lower midsection in the center, with the heel of the hand. The weight shifts to the forward foot; the wrist snaps and the hand rolls over the top of the ball, imparting a top spinning action.

The method of getting direction on the overhand spin serve is exactly the same as for the underhand. The server may face the direction he wishes to hit the ball, and contact the ball in the center, or he may face the net, and contact the ball on the lower left or right side.

Common errors in the spinning serve are: 1) *Hitting the ball into the net.* This is caused by allowing the ball to drop too low on the toss, and contacting it on the top. You must reach with your arm almost fully extended and contact on the lower half of the ball. 2) *Hitting the ball to the right.* This is caused by tossing the ball too far outside the right shoulder. You must be sure to keep the ball directly in front of your shoulder. 3) *Hitting the ball to the left.* This is caused by tossing the ball too much in the center of your body, thus causing your arm to swing across your body to contact the ball.

Learning Experience: Spinning Serve

Stand 10 to 15 feet from a wall. Can you hit the ball above an 8 foot line, imparting a spinning action to the ball?

Increase the distance to 20 feet. Draw two vertical lines on the wall spaced 10 feet apart. Above the 8 foot line, draw a line 4 feet above and parallel to it. Can you control the serve enough to place it between the two vertical and parallel lines? As you gain the control necessary, increase your distance from the wall.

Learning Experience: Spinning Serve, Over Net

Stand behind the baseline, in the serving area, and hit the ball over the net. Can you hit 10 balls over the net so that they "drop" into the court with a spinning action?

Can you control this action by serving it to various predetermined areas of the court?

Place a rope 4 feet above and parallel to the net. Can you serve the ball under the rope into the court? How many times out of 10 serves? As control is gained, decrease the space between the rope and net.

2. The pass, which is the first touch of the ball on the receiving side, puts the defensive team on the offense.

The receiving team must be able to place the ball to an advantageous spot on the court in order to set up an offensive play. There are two basic passes: the *overhand pass* and the *forearm pass*, or *bump*.

2a. The overhand pass is the most accurate method used to control an easy or "free" ball coming over the net. A *free ball* is one that is returned easily over the net in an upward trajectory by the opponents because of an error in technique. The overhand pass is a much more controlled technique because the player has contact with the ball with the fingers of both hands, has the ball between his eyes and his intended target, and can put the ball exactly where he wants it with much more consistency.

The preliminary stance for receiving the free ball is with the feet in a stride position, either right or left foot in front, or both feet parallel, knees slightly bent, trunk erect, weight on the balls of the feet, hands up and eyes on the ball.

The most important factor in receiving a moving ball is to move quickly into position directly behind the ball so that the ball will drop in front of you. You should be standing still, facing the direction you wish to pass the ball. The hands should be up, about four to six inches in front of your eyes and forehead, with the thumbs and index fingers forming a triangle, and the elbows bent slightly outward at about shoulder level. Fingers are spread and cupped, and wrists hyperextended so that you can see the ball and the back of your hands (Fig. 2.3).

Contact the ball just above and in front of your eyes with the fleshy part of the last finger joint. Upon contact, the knees and arms extend simultaneously and the wrists extend. The ball is contacted just below the

Figure 2.3. Overhand Passing

midsection, and should be arched high into the air to give the setter time to get underneath it. On the follow-through, the knees and arms are fully extended and the passer's body and feet are pointing in the direction of flight.

Common errors and corrections in passing are: 1) *The pass is considered by the official to be a thrown ball.* This can occur when the player does not get good position, with the ball in the center of the body and the shoulders directly under or behind the ball. The player therefore tries to direct the ball by "carrying" it with his hands and arms from the original point of contact, across the body, to the point of release. This is an infraction of the rules, which state that a ball that remains in contact with the hands longer than momentarily is a "carried" or "thrown" ball. 2) *The pass goes straight ahead with no height to the ball.* Usually the player is too far behind the ball and allows it to drop too low before contact. 3) *The pass goes behind the player's head.* This, too, is caused by incorrect body positioning, with the player contacting the ball too far over his head. It is essential that the passer learn to get to the ball with his body completely behind it, seeing the ball, the back of his hands, and the intended target.

Learning Experience: Body Positioning

Stand facing a partner about 15 feet away. Suspend a rope between the two partners, about 12 to 15 feet high. The partner tosses the ball high in the air, about 4 to 5 feet to the passer's left. The passer runs to the left, behind the ball, stops, faces the partner and passes the ball back over the rope.

Can you complete an accurate pass moving both to your left and your right? Increase the distance of the throw to the left and right to about 6 to 8 feet. How many passes out of 10 can you return to your partner that can be caught with two hands above the head, and the movement of only one foot?

Learning Experience: Use of Wrists, Arms and Body

Stand about 2 feet from a wall. Pass the ball very rapidly against the wall, just above eye level. Can you do this with minimum body motion, using just arms or just wrists? Move away to a distance of about 3 to 4 feet. Can you still pass the ball to a height of 8 to 10 feet with just your arms?

Move 6 to 8 feet away and pass the ball 15 feet high. Do you find it necessary to push the ball with all your body force?

Learning Experience: Receiving the Free Ball Over the Net

Stand in the center of the court about three-fourths of the length from the net. A partner stands on the opposite side of the net and throws the ball underhand directly to you. Can you pass the ball 12 to 15 feet into the air and have the ball land in an area 10' × 10' marked in the center of the court next to the center line?

Next have your partner force you to move for his free ball. Can you get behind the ball in time to stop, face your target, pass the ball 12 to 15 feet high, and have it land in the marked area? How many times out of 10 tries?

2b. The forearm (or bump) pass is used to handle low balls and hard spikes and serves. The forearm pass has become more widely used because the receiver is less likely to be called for an illegal hit.

As in the overhand pass, the body should be directly behind the ball with the feet in a stride position, knees bent and the trunk slightly forward. The hands should be extended away from the body, about knee high. Some players prefer placing the back of one hand in the palm of the other, with the thumbs parallel (see Fig. 2.4A). Another popular method is the *clenched* fist position (see Fig. 2.4B). This hand position presents a good rebounding surface for balls that cannot be reached with the forearms and must be struck with the hands. In both positions the arms are fully extended in a line parallel with the thighs, with the elbows rotated outward, so that the flat inner surface of the forearm creates a rigid rebound surface. The elbows are locked by forcing the wrists to point at a 45° angle to the floor and the eyes remain on the ball. Once this

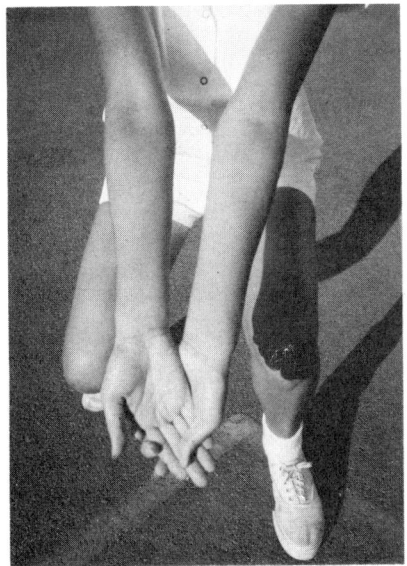 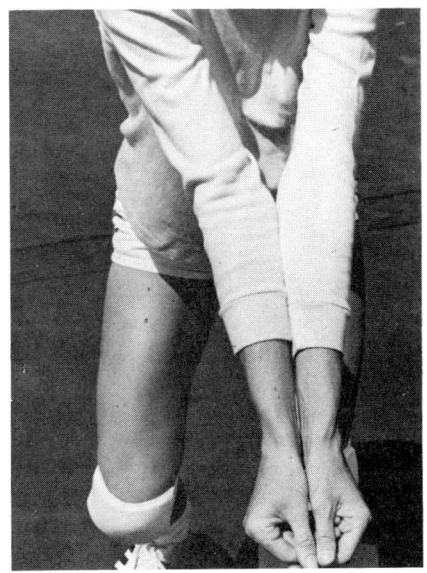

Photographs courtesy of Los Angeles Unified School District

A. Thumb Over Fingers   B. Clenched Fist

Figure 2.4. Hand and Arm Position on Bump

position is assumed, the movement of the arms is directed in an arc from the shoulders.

As the ball is contacted, the entire body functions as a unit and the knees straighten as the body gives impetus to the ball. As the knees straighten and the body extends, the ball seemingly remains in contact with the forearms, thus giving greater control to the pass. The ball should be contacted about waist high, directly in front of the body. A common mistake by many beginners is moving the arms in a downward and upward motion without bending and extending the knees.

The body follow-through depends upon the impetus needed to control the ball. If the ball moves over the net slowly, it would need to be contacted with more of an upward thrust from the legs and body in order to propel it high into the air. On the other hand, if it were a hard driven spike, the digger would want to "buffer" the impact of the ball by falling back, imparting no follow-through—as a batter might do when bunting a baseball.

Common errors and corrections in bumping are: 1) *The ball rebounds from the arms at different angles and with no control.* This usually happens because the digger is swinging at the ball, is not directly underneath it or contacts it on the fists. It is essential to keep the elbows locked, with the movement of the arms coming from the shoulders. The ball should be contacted directly in front of the body, with the forearms. The feet should be shoulder-width apart, with one foot slightly in front of

Figure 2.5. The Bump Pass

the other. 2) *The ball does not rebound high enough into the air.* This is caused by a person not using his entire body. Upon contact, his knees should straighten and his trunk and arms come upward with as much force as necessary to get the ball up.

Learning Experience: Using Body to Bump

Stand behind a line drawn 4 to 6 feet from a wall. Can you bump a ball between two lines marked on the wall at 10 feet and 14 feet . . . 10, 15, and 20 times in succession?

ESSENTIAL SKILLS FOR POWER VOLLEYBALL

Repeat this, limiting your lateral movement to within a two-foot distance.

Can you stand inside the free throw circle on a basketball court and bump the ball 10, 15 or 20 times in succession to the height of the basket?

Stand 20 feet from the net. A partner stands on the opposite side of the net and tosses the ball over the net to you. Can you bump the ball over a rope 12 feet high placed on the court 11½ feet from the net?

When you can achieve this 5 or 6 times out of 10; add a target 10' × 10' placed in the middle of the court next to the center line. Can you bump the ball over the rope into this square? How many times out of 10 attempts?

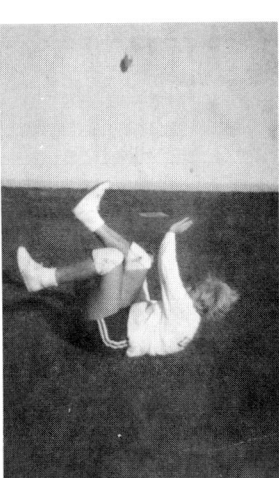

Figure 2.6. Digging a Hard Driven Spike

Learning Experience: Receiving the Serve

Repeat the same drill as described for the bump; only now have the partner stand behind the end line and serve the ball.

Begin with an easy underhand serve, and progress to the overhand as the skill is mastered. A minimum score of 5 or 6 correct passes should be required before progressing on to the more difficult serves; the overhand spin, and the floater.

Is there any difference in receiving the spin serve versus the floater serve? How do they affect your positioning and follow-through?

3. The set is placed high in the air, close to the net, so as to be hit down into the opponents' court with maximum force.

It is essential that this skill be well executed, therefore the set-up player or setter on a team should be one of the best ball handlers. It is the setter's responsibility to receive the pass and then place the ball in the air close to the net to the advantage of the spiker. The ball is usually placed from 4 to 10 feet above the net, one to two feet away from the net, and to the outside right or left front corners.

There are two setters on a team, who play diagonally opposite one another, *i.e.*, left front and right back, so that one setter is always in the front row. The starting position of the front row setter is close to the net, with the side of his body toward the net. This takes him out of the serve-receiving pattern, leaving him free to move to receive the pass. The pass, ideally, should be to a designated spot about two to four feet from the net.

When the ball is served, the setter starts to move to the designated spot for the pass, usually the center front. Assuming that the serve receiver makes a perfect pass, the setter positions his body with his side facing the net, feet planted firmly on the floor, knees bent and hands up. The pass will travel across the center of his body and the ball will be contacted above and in front of his eyes, as in the overhand pass. The setter may position his body so as to set the ball to the spiker on either side. If his body is facing the direction of the intended set, then his knees merely straighten and his arms follow through, allowing his body to move with the set. When the setter moves with the set, he is able to "back-up" the spiker in order to retrieve the spiked ball that rebounds back into the court off the defensive blocker's hands.

If the pass is not perfect and the setter is forced to run back away from the net, some adjustments must be made. As was mentioned above, the setter always moves with his side to the net. If the pass is close to the net, the setter's body is at right angles to the net, as shown in Fig. 2.8. The farther away from the net the setter must move for the pass, the more the right angle to the net decreases, and the more his body faces the net (see Fig. 2.8). The setter never moves toward the pass by directly facing the serve receiver, but merely faces the side of the court to which the ball is served and moves with his side toward the serve receiver.

For example, if the serve is coming over the net hard and the receiver is forced deep into the court, the setter should face the side of the court to which the ball is served and move toward the receiver. The more difficult the serve is to receive, the more the setter should anticipate a pass that may not reach the net. The setter may move with side-step sliding movements to keep his side toward the net, and face the direction of the intended set. If the setter cannot possibly reach the pass, another player must call him off, and step in and set the ball.

Figure 2.7. The Set

To set a low pass (see Fig. 2.9) the player's buttocks are close to the floor and hands are in front of his face. The back is straight at contact and the weight is centered behind the back foot.

Common errors and corrections in setting are: 1) *The most common error in beginning setters is that they approach the ball facing the passer, and therefore never get behind the ball so as to face the direction they intend to set.* The flight and speed of the moving ball must be considered. As the pass reaches the height of its arc, it will drop at the same angle at which it rose. The setter must therefore learn to judge this. If the setter is forced to move away from the net, he must actually run beyond the ball

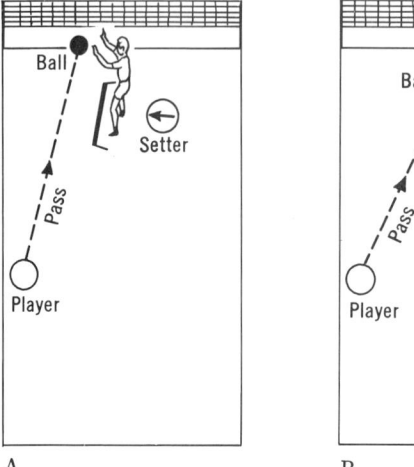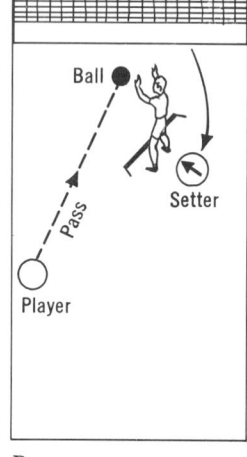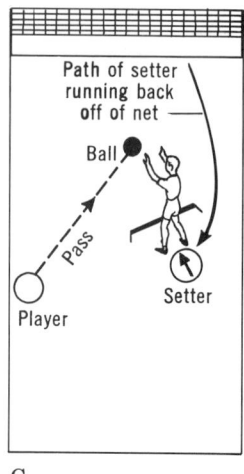

Figure 2.8. Body Position

Figure 2.9. Setting a Low Pass

Photographs courtesy of the Ealing Corporation

so that as he faces toward his intended target, the ball is between him and the net, in the center of his body. If he is behind the ball, he will not have to reach right or left to contact it as he sets it up to the net (see Fig.

2.8C). 2) *The beginning setter tries to set the ball while on the run.* The setter must move quickly to get to the ball in time to stop. He must make his move quickly, to get behind the ball while it is in its upward flight, making any minor adjustment necessary on its descent. 3) *The setter does not push the ball high enough or wide enough to the sidelines, close to the net.* Usually the setter is not following through with his legs and body to get enough momentum on the ball. In order to get any distance or height on the ball, a setter must use his entire body to follow through, instead of merely extending his arms.

Learning Experience: Body Positioning for Setting

Suspend two parallel ropes at a height of 14½ feet to 16 feet. Place a starting line on the floor 8 feet from and parallel to the ropes. Measure a distance of 15½ feet from the ropes and place a target 2 feet square on the floor in a direct line with the starting line. For testing purposes a target 2' × 10' with the center of the target the perfect landing point, should be used.

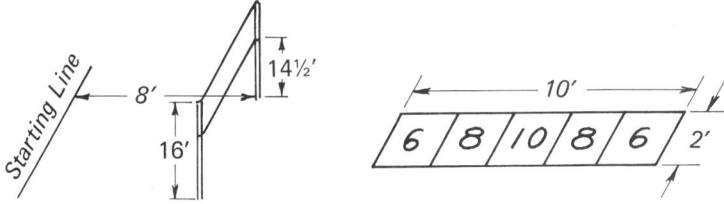

The student stands behind the starting line, tosses the ball to himself, and overhand sets the ball between the ropes into the target area. For the purposes of scoring or testing, numbers should be assigned to each 2 foot square of the target; the highest being assigned to the center. These numbers, or points, allow for some error in the force and distance of the ball flight.

How many points can you score out of 10 attempts?

Learning Experience: Setting the Pass

Place three people across the court to receive the serve. Setter stands at the net. Server serves underhand. Setter receives the pass from the receiver and sets the ball to the side of the court from which the ball is served. How many good sets can you make out of 10 passes?

---

4. The spike is a powerful offensive play that drives the ball down into the opponents' court with great force; it requires a coordinated approach, jump, and armswing at the moving ball.

The spiker places the ball into the opponents' court with such force that it is difficult or impossible to return.

For right- or left-handed spikers, there are easier and more difficult spikes to perform, depending upon which side of the court the ball is set to. These are called "on-hand" and "off-hand" spikes. The "on-hand" side of the court is the side on which the spiker would contact the ball with his predominant hand before it would cross in front of his body. For example, the left front corner would be the "on-hand" side for a right-handed spiker, as the ball would be contacted in front of his right shoulder. Conversely, if the ball were set to the right front corner, it would have to travel across his body to the right side before the spiker could contact the ball. This is more difficult to perform, and is known as the "off-hand" spike. For the left-handed spiker, the "on-hand" and "off-hand" sides of the court are reversed—"off-hand" being the left front, and "on-hand" being the right front.

The preliminary position for the left front spiker is approximately 8 to 12 feet from the net, on or outside the left sideline. The head is turned toward the ball, consequently the left shoulder is facing the net—the correct position for the approach. The spiker, by watching the play, is able to adjust his position to that of the setters, so as to approach the ball at an angle.

Using three or more steps, the spiker approaches the ball at an angle, keeping the ball an arm's distance in front and on the right side of his

A. On-Hand

B. Off-Hand

Figure 2.10. Spiking Positions

Photographs courtesy of Stan Abraham

ESSENTIAL SKILLS FOR POWER VOLLEYBALL

Figure 2.11. Step-Close Takeoff

body. There are two variations to the approach. In the step-close takeoff (Fig. 2.11), the spiker takes the last step by jumping more forward than upward, contacting the floor with the heel of one foot first and then the heel of the second foot; his weight then rolls from both heels to the toes as he takes the jump. In the hop approach, the take-off is from one foot

Figure 2.12. Hop Takeoff

Figure 2.13. The Spike

up into the air, landing with both heels simultaneously; the weight then shifts forward to the balls of his feet (Fig. 2.12). In both approaches, as his heels hit the ground his knees bend and his arms swing behind him. As his weight shifts forward from the heels to the balls of the feet his legs straighten, his arms thrust upward, his back arches and his body is behind the ball, with his shoulders parallel to the net. As his right arm bends (in a throwing motion), his left arm drops and his left shoulder rotates toward the net. The spiking hand is held open, with either a cupped or a very flat and stiff hand, and with the elbow up. The spiker then swings rapidly at the ball, leading with his elbow, extending his arm and contacting the ball with his open hand. At contact, his wrist snaps vigorously over the ball. At the same time, his whole upper trunk snaps forward from the waist.

After contact, his arm must swing away from his body so that the net will not be struck. If the ball comes back after the block, the spiker must immediately back away from the net, to be ready for another approach. If the ball remains on the opponents's side, he stays at the net to block.

When teaching beginners, a device called a Spike It (Fig. 2.14) has proven valuable because it allows the athlete to concentrate on his approach and armswing in a controlled learning situation.

Common errors in spiking are: 1) *Most beginners approach the ball too soon, and therefore either find themselves underneath the ball, or find the ball behind them.* The spiker must always keep himself behind the ball, therefore he must wait until the ball leaves the setter's hands before he starts his approach. 2) *The beginning spiker does not get any power on the ball.* This usually occurs when he does not keep the ball in front of his right shoulder, and therefore gets no shoulder turn. He may be approaching with his right shoulder already toward the net, or he may allow the ball to get past his right shoulder to the center of his body, forcing him to hit with his right shoulder—rather than his left—toward the net. He also may not be utilizing a vigorous wrist snap when contacting the ball. 3) *Spiking the ball long and out of the court is another common*

Figure 2.14. The Spike It

Photo courtesy of Dennis Keller

fault. This is usually caused when the player is too far under the ball and is contacting it on the bottom or below the midsection. 4) *Hitting the ball into the net is a fault not only of beginners, but also of many advanced players.* This is caused by attempting to hit the ball straight down into the opponents's court, or by jumping too late and contacting the ball too low on the set. The ball must be contacted with the arm extended, or with the elbow bent slightly. One must also learn to judge the exact time to jump in order to hit the ball at the correct height.

Learning Experience: Wrist Snap

Hold the ball in your free hand. With your spiking hand open, contact the ball at the top with a forceful wrist snap. Does the ball hit the floor and rebound vertically into the air? Can you get the ball to rebound 20 to 25 feet in the air?

Learning Experience: Position of Ball
In Relation to Shoulder

Stand on a line 20 feet from a wall. Place two parallel lines 2 feet apart extending perpendicular from the wall to the starting line. Spiker stands behind the starting line, squarely facing the wall with the spiking arm normally extended (not stretching) overhead. Partner holds a ball directly in front of the hitting shoulder at a height that the fingertips of the extended arm touch the bottom of the ball. Having established the proper ball height for the particular spiker, the spiker starts with both feet flat on the ground, and arms down. The spiker swings rapidly at the ball making contact with an open hand at the midsection. If struck correctly, the ball should land between the two parallel lines, in an area one foot from the wall on the floor, to one foot above the floor on the wall.

In order to make proper contact on the ball, the spiker must extend the reach by lateral flexion of the upper trunk. The force in the spike comes from the movement of the upper trunk from hyperextension to flexion, from medial rotation of the shoulder, and flexion of the wrist. The direction comes from hand contact directly in the midsection of the ball as it is held in front of the hitting shoulder and between the two parallel lines.

How many times out of 10 attempts does the ball hit in the proper area?

Repeat the same drill, but add an approach and a jump. Partner now stands on a chair; height of the ball determined by a standing jump of the spiker, with the bottom of the ball still held at fingertip reach.

How many times out of 10 does the ball hit in the proper area? Do you, the spiker, remain behind the 20 foot starting line after the jump?

Repeat this drill at the net. Can you hit the ball without touching the net, or going under the center line? How many hits out of 10 can you direct down the line?

How many hits out of 10 can you direct crosscourt?

Learning Experience: Hitting a Controlled Set

Have a setter stand at the net, holding the ball, while you stand about 8 or 10 feet from the net. When he tosses the ball high into the air, start your approach. Can you hit the ball in the court 7 out of 10 times?

Next, have the spiker start with the ball 10 feet from the net and pass it to the setter. After the set, make your approach and hit the ball. Can you spike to your opponent's left back corner, to his right back corner and to the center of the court 7 out of 10 times?

The same principle used in serving applies for spiking the ball in different directions. The ball should be struck off-center in order to achieve the various angles of flight.

The preliminary position for approaching the "off-hand" spike is the same as for the "on-hand," but from the opposite side of the court.

It is more difficult to hit from the right side of the net, since the ball must cross in front of your body to your right side and your left shoulder must face the net. If the setter does not push the ball out to the sideline, the hitter should move toward the center of the court, so as to allow the ball to cross his body.

5. The best defense against the spike is for one or more players to leap near the net and block the ball just after it is hit.

After your team serves the ball, every effort should be made to prevent the offense from putting the ball down on your side of the court. The best way to accomplish this is with an attack block. Blockers should reach as far over the net as possible and block the spike before it crosses the net. When the ball is set close to the net this method is extremely effective. The blockers should time their jump so that their bodies are at maximum height or just beginning to descent when the ball is contacted by the spiker. Their fingers should be spread over or around the ball and held rigid. In most situations there will be a two-man block, and occasionally a one- or three-man block (Fig. 2.15).

Top three photographs courtesy of Stan Troutman

A. One-Man   B. Two-Man   C. Three-Man

Figure 2.15. The Block

Lower three photographs courtesy of Stan Abraham

How do you demoralize a team? By not allowing their star spiker to hit the ball over the net. In Fig. 2.16, the spiker has just had a hard-driven ball knocked back into his face before he has returned to the floor. Hard-hitting spikers find it increasingly difficult to put the ball away as the opposition realizes the importance of aligning their best blockers against them. Often a good block will score over 50 percent of a team's points—either indirectly, by intimidating their opponents to use poor percentage shots to avoid the block, or directly, by blocking balls for a point.

In the basic position, the left and right outside blockers should usually start about two feet from the sideline, with the middle blocker standing halfway between them (Fig. 2.17A). After the ball leaves the setter's fingertips, the blockers watch the attacking spiker and converge on him to form the ready position (Fig. 2.17B) for the normal two-man block. In the ready position, the blocker may be anywhere from six inches to four

ESSENTIAL SKILLS FOR POWER VOLLEYBALL

Figure 2.16. Blocking for a Point

Photo courtesy of Stan Troutman

feet from the net, depending on his height and jumping ability. Short blockers or poor jumpers usually start farther away from the net so they can utilize an armswing to increase their jumping height. Tall persons with a good jump should stand six to twelve inches from the net, with their

A. Starting Position

B. Ready Position

Figure 2.17. Blocking Position

Photographs courtesy of Stan Troutman

feet shoulder-width apart, body and forearms parallel to the net and hands held face high. All blockers should eventually jump close to the net, with their forearms parallel to or over the net.

When the blocker is confident he can be in front of the attacking spiker before he jumps, the slide step should be used to close the gap between blockers. This is similar to the basic defensive step in basketball, in that the blocker does not cross his legs. It is slower than the cross-over step, but it enables the blocker to stay close to the net in the ready position, with his hands held up and his body and forearms parallel to the net. The slide step also prevents the blockers from crashing into one another and permits a better view of the approaching spiker. The faster, traditional approach for the center blocker is the cross-over step, which should be used on low wide sets or anytime the blocker gets a late start on the ball. Blockers using the cross-over step must concentrate on turning parallel to the net when they arrive at the block. Blockers use the cross-over step by instinct, but they may feel awkward at the slide step until they have practiced it a great deal.

Learning Experience: Blocking Steps

Face your partner on the opposite side of the net, in the ready position. Jump and clap his hands over the net. Slide to the center and to the other side of the court, and repeat. Continue the drill, using the cross-over step. Can you contact your partner's hands on his side of the net? Can you use an armswing while jumping, without touching the net?

Learning Experience: Blocking In The Middle Position

Stand at the net in the middle of the court, facing two opposing spikers and a setter. One of the spikers passes the ball to the setter, who delivers a high wide set to either spiker.

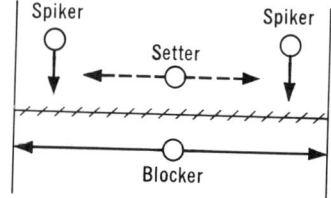

Figure 2.18. Blocking Drill

Your responsibility is to block the spike. Can you move into good blocking position using the slide step? The cross-over step? Can the setter force you to move in the wrong direction and miss the block? Can you move into good blocking position for nine out of ten spikes? Can you block three out of ten spikes?

The blocker moves in the direction of the set until he closes to within an arm's length of the player responsible for positioning the block. The blocker who positions the block places himself in such a manner that the ball will be spaced between him and his teammate when the spiker attacks it. The outside blocker's primary responsibility is to position the block on wide sets, and the middle blocker's to position the block on inside sets; the blockers should align themselves so they can each take half the ball on their inside hands by moving their arms laterally after the attacking spiker has committed himself. When the ball is set to the center spiker, the outside blocker joins the middle blocker. This enables the defense to use normal backcourt coverage. Occasionally all three frontcourt players block the center spiker; however, if the ball gets by the block there are only three men left to cover the entire court.

The tall blocker or good jumper should never be more than a foot away from the net prior to jumping. This usually ensures a tight block and enables the blocker to wait longer before declaring himself to the spiker. The tall blocker should not have to use a full armswing to increase the height of his jump, since this maneuver increases the likelihood of hitting the net. He simply extends his arms up and over the net from the ready position as he jumps. Superior jumpers will be able to extend their forearms and elbows over the net, while the great majority of blockers will be able only to keep their forearms close to the tape at the top of the net and reach over with their wrists and hands. Blockers should experiment with the three-quarter and full squat in an attempt to increase their jumping height. If a blocker still cannot jump high enough, he should start a step or two away from the net and use a full armswing. This technique should be used only by poor jumpers or short blockers, because of the tendency of the blocker to hit the net or cross the centerline.

The easiest balls to block are those set within a foot of the net. Blockers should reach over the net and "roof" the close set by placing their hands over and around the ball, leaving the spiker in a hopeless situation.

Average blockers cannot jump high enough to roof balls that are set 18 inches or more away from the net, so they must rely on their ability to judge the intentions of the spiker. A less aggressive or *soft block* should be used by most players when the ball is set deeper than five feet from the net. The forearms and hands are held parallel and very close to the net. The blocker attempts to intercept the ball with the hands as it starts to cross the net. Small blockers and middle blockers who are slow to arrive at the point of attack often use the soft block. The end or outside blockers may choose to use the soft block when balls are set outside the court, to prevent the spiker from ricocheting the ball off the block and out-of-bounds.

Knowing and eliminating common errors commited in the block will strengthen a player's defense. Common errors in the block are: 1) *Touching the net.* This can be caused by: a) broad jumping on the approach—you should jump straight up into the air; b) using an armswing while jumping—increase the height of your jump through weight training, so that an armswing will not be necessary; c) reaching too far over the net—you must learn your safe range of motion when blocking, and stick to it. 2) *The ball bouncing down the front of your body on your side of the court.* This can be caused by: a) starting the jump too far from the net and by jumping before the attacker does; b) being late on the block—time your jump just a fraction of a second after the attacker's. 3) *Constantly missing the spike.* This is caused by: a) dipping your head or closing your eyes—you should know why every ball went past your block, so if you cannot do this, force yourself to keep your eyes on the ball; b) watching the ball instead of the spiker—primary attention should be focused on the approaching spiker, as the ball will come into view as it nears the spiker; c) not having learned to judge the spiker's approach—at least move your block around until you take away his strongest shots; d) blocking too wide—take more of the crosscourt angle away from the spiker. 4) *The ball ricocheting off your hands and out of play.* This is caused by: a) using the flat surface of your hands or forearms, instead of turning the ball in by angling your hands and arms toward the spiker; b) attempting to block a wide set too aggressively, instead of deflecting it to a teammate.

OUTCOMES

After studying this chapter, you should be able to:

1. State how the ball is put into play, and why it is important to perfect this technique.
2. Name the three types of serves.
3. Hit underhand serves so that they land in the opposite court.
4. Describe and demonstrate the easiest way for a beginner to serve to different areas of the court.
5. Describe and demonstrate how the above skill may be achieved without "giving away" the intended direction of the serve.
6. Hit underhand serves so that they land in selected areas of the court.
7. Explain why underhand serves hit the net, go too high in the air, or too long or wide in the opposite court; and explain what can be done to correct these errors.
8. Explain what characteristics of the "floater" serve make it difficult to handle by the defensive team.

ESSENTIAL SKILLS FOR POWER VOLLEYBALL

9. Explain and demonstrate how the ball is held and hit so that it crosses the net with a "wiggle" type action.
10. Hit several floater serves into specific areas of the opposite court with reasonable consistency in placement and ball action.
11. Describe the common error made in executing the floater serve and what can be done to correct it.
12. Tell what characteristic of the overhand spin serve makes it harder to receive than the underhand serve.
13. Describe how to hit the overhand spin serve to various sections of the court, and demonstrate several with regular consistency.
14. Explain how to correct three errors commonly made in hitting the overhand spin serve.
15. State the purpose of a pass.
16. State the most important aspect of receiving a moving ball.
17. List the advantages and disadvantages of the overhand pass.
18. Explain and demonstrate the technique of making an overhand pass.
19. Explain how to correct common errors made in executing this pass.
20. Receive several balls and execute an overhand pass so that they go high in the air and land in a designated area of your court.
21. Explain why the "bump" or "dig" pass is being more widely used today.
22. Describe and demonstrate the position and movement of the hands, arms, and body when making a "dig" pass.
23. Explain how the speed of the oncoming ball affects the body movement in executing this pass.
24. Receive several balls at various speeds directed at or in front of your body, and hit them with a two-handed dig so that they go high and land in a designated area of your court.
25. Explain the principle of body positioning common to both the overhand pass and the dig pass.
26. List some causes of the uncontrolled dig pass and describe how to correct them.
27. Demonstrate a good set.
28. Explain why the front row setter stands at the net on serve reception.
29. Demonstrate the position of the setter's body when setting a perfect pass.
30. When moving away from the net for a pass, describe the relationship between the setter's body, the ball and the intended direction of the set.
31. State the setter's immediate job as soon as the ball is set.
32. Explain why the spike is so difficult to master.

33. Demonstrate the "on-hand" spike.
34. Demonstrate the "off-hand" spike.
35. Explain why the off-hand spike is more difficult to hit.
36. State why the spiker should start his approach back from the net.
37. Demonstrate how the spiker should approach the ball.
38. Explain how the spiker knows when to start his approach.
39. Spike a ball down the line and crosscourt, using the same approach.
40. Define the basic position and the ready position in the block.
41. Demonstrate the slide step and the cross-over step, and explain the situations in which they should be used.
42. State when a blocker should use an armswing.
43. Demonstrate a three-quarter and full squat and jump from the ready position. Repeat, using an armswing.
44. Demonstrate how to "roof" a spiked ball.
45. Explain when a soft block should be used.
46. List three reasons why blockers contact the net.
47. List several errors that may cause blockers to miss the ball.

3

Volleyball Rules

CONCEPT: There is a worldwide trend toward standardization of volleyball rules at all levels of competition.

In this country the United States Volleyball Association (USVBA) has been the rule-making body for all men's and women's competition at the national and regional levels. Most coeducational and recreational leagues are also governed by this USVBA body.

The Division for Girls' and Women's Sports (DGWS) of the American Association for Health, Physical Education and Recreation (AAHPER) publishes a set of rules used for most intramural, interscholastic, and intercollegiate competition for girls and women. Every two years, the DGWS rules are revised. The AAHPER and the USVBA established a Joint Committee on Volleyball in 1967. Since then the DGWS and USVBA rules are moving closer.

The International Volleyball Federation also publishes a set of rules, which is automatically adopted by all other countries in the world and used for all international competition including the Olympics.

With the acceptance of volleyball into the Olympic Games and our increased competition with foreign countries, the USVBA has adopted most of the rules of the International Volleyball Federation and retained some of the better American rules. Therefore, all teams in this country that play in open competition will play under the "Official Rules" of the USVBA, which are the same as slightly modified international rules. The NCAA, NAIA and NJCAA also use USVBA "Official Rules".

1. The playing area is divided into two courts by a net, each court having a serving area and a spiking line.

The volleyball playing area measures 60 feet by 30 feet, and it is divided into two equal courts by a centerline, which is 4 inches wide.

The service area is marked by extension lines six inches long from the right sideline to an area ten feet from the sideline. There should be a minimum of six feet behind the service line and around the court, and an area 26 feet high above the court, free from all obstructions. (A height of 30 feet or more is recommended.)

There is also an additional line extending parallel to and ten feet from the net, called an *attacking line.* This line governs the back row player rule of jumping to hit the ball over the net.

The height of the net is 8' for men, and 7'4¼" for women. The ball is made of leather, is 25" to 27" in circumference and weighs not less than 250 grams or more than 280 grams.

2. A match consists of the best two out of three games.

The team winning the coin toss chooses either service or side, the loser getting the alternate choice. The teams alternate this first service every other game. If the match goes to the third game, the teams shall automatically change playing areas after: 1) one team has scored eight points, or 2) the first time the ball becomes dead after four minutes of ball in play. NCAA, NAIA, and NJCAA matches consist of the best three out of five games with no time limit.

3. Both teams must be lined up in their correct rotation order before the serve.

The players in both lines, in order to remain in correct rotation order, must not overlap with the feet of the players immediately to their right or left. The back row players must be in their proper area with relation to those on either side, but they may line up in any manner in relation to the front row, as long as they are behind their respective front line players at the instant the ball is served. For example, if the center front player moved up close to the net (Fig. 3.1), then the center back player could stand even with or in front of the remaining front row players, as long as he remained behind the center front player.

4. The ball is put in play by the right back player from the right third of the back line.

The game and service are started by a whistle from the referee. Tossing the ball in the air and contacting it immediately as the whistle blows shall not be allowed by the referee, since the rules state that the serve is initiated only after the whistle.

5. After the serve, players may exchange positions on the court within their respective lines.

Back and front row players do not change positions, as the back row player may not block or jump at the net. The front row players might wish to switch positions so that the shorter blocker would be blocking the

VOLLEYBALL RULES

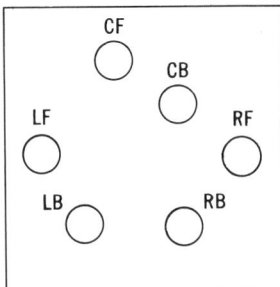

Figure 3.1. Offensive Positioning

opponents' shorter man or weaker hitter. The back row players might switch so the best defensive digger is crosscourt from the opponents' best spiker, and so on. This allows both the offensive and defensive teams to move their players to the positions suited for their individual capabilities and for the best all-around team strength.

6. The ball must be clearly hit.

The official interpretation of a "thrown" or "guided" ball on the first pass has necessitated the use of the forearm pass or bump for receiving serves and controlling the ball from a spike. If the ball remains momentarily in the hands, or makes a loud sound on the overhand pass, the referee will usually call a *foul*. Even when the ball is hit with the forearms, it must be contacted cleanly without rolling up the arms or being hit twice.

Once the ball has been passed, the current interpretation allows more leniency on the set and on the "dink" (a guided shot by the spiker over the net). For example, the ball does not have to travel in the direction the body is facing as long as there is an immediate contact and release with little or no follow-through by the hands and arms. This interpretation allows a little more deception on the part of the setter and spiker in outmaneuvering the blockers.

As long as contact is made on his side of the net, the spiker may follow through with his hand and arm over the net. On the dink, the spiker is usually allowed to change the course of the ball by directing it across his body, if the change of direction does not come from a break or follow-through of his wrist.

7. Although players may reach over the net in following-through or blocking the ball, they may not touch the net or cross into the opposite court until the ball is dead.

The defensive blockers may reach over the net to contact the ball if they do not touch the ball before the offensive player has attacked it. The blockers may contact the ball again if it is deflected on their own side, even if there is only one person blocking. The blocker may spike or intentionally place the ball over the net on this second contact, or set it to a teammate.

The players at the net are not allowed to contact the net. Touching the opponents' court with a foot or feet is not a fault, providing that some part of the encroaching foot or feet remains on or above the centerline at the time of such contact. It is not a fault to enter the opponent's court after the whistle has blown. A player at the net who is off balance may cross the center line near the sideline by going under the net and landing out-of-bounds on the opponents' side, without constituting a foul.

8. The ball may be hit three times by a team before it crosses the net.

When the attacking team hits the ball over the net, the ball becomes *dead* by touching the floor or by being hit out of play or played illegally. The ball remains in play by being dug by the defensive team or successfully blocked back into the attacker's court. Once a team plays the ball on their side, they will usually take the three hits allowed them in order to set the ball and spike it over the net. A player who is touched by the ball shall be considered as having played the ball. If two players go for the ball and it is obviously contacted by only one, it shall be considered as one hit. If, however, two people go for the ball and both of them contact it, or appear to the official to have contacted it, it will be considered as two hits. The ball may be contacted only by the part of the body above and including the waist.

9. Back row players may not spike the ball in front of the 10-foot line.

If a player in the back row is hitting the ball over the net, he may not jump and contact the ball unless he begins his jump from behind the attacking line, which is 10 feet from the net and parallel to it. A back row player who is in front of the 10-foot line may not leave the floor, nor contact the ball at a height above the height of the net when hitting the ball over the net. Obviously, a back line player may not spike at the net.

10. Substitutes may reenter a game twice, with a maximum of 12 substitutions permitted.

When a substitution is made, the player entering the game must do so immediately. The player leaving the game and the one entering must acknowledge this change by reporting to the scorekeeper, so that the numbers of the players involved can be recorded. If a player is not ready to enter the game at the time the substitution is called, a team *time-out* is charged.

VOLLEYBALL RULES

A team consists of six players on the court and a total squad of no more than twelve. Since injuries, errors, and "off" or ineffective days for some players occur, and since personal weaknesses of individuals must be considered, substitutions become a very important part of overall team effectiveness. A maximum of 12 substitutions can be made in each game. A player starting a game may be substituted and reenter twice, and a substitute may enter and reenter twice.

In order to make proper substitutions at the correct time, it is important for a coach to know the strengths and weaknesses of his entire squad. If, for instance, the best spiker and blocker at the net is a weak defensive player in the back court, this player should be substituted in the right back position and returned to the game in the left front position. Similarly, a team may have an excellent back court player who is a weak blocker. If the game is approaching a crucial situation where a point or two could make the difference between victory or defeat, and the opponents are scoring over this weak blocker, he should be substituted. However, when a player substitutes at the net he should have the same offensive capabilities as that of the player he replaces: that is, a setter for a setter, and a spiker for a spiker. In the back row this is not necessarily true, since defense is the key and the offensive responsibility of the player is not the criterion for substitution.

Since there are only 12 substitutions allowed during a game, the coach should substitute strategically. For example, the coach should gauge the tempo of the game and make the substitution when the best spiker is tired. At this point, the spiker would probably play his weakest defensive game across the backcourt. Also, the spiker needs the rest in order to be strong enough to reenter and score the final necessary points. A coach must be careful not to use all of his substitutions too soon, because when the game gets down to the last few vital points he may then want to make an important change. In DGWS rules a player shall not enter the game for the third time; starting the game counts as an entry.

11. A team is allowed two time-outs, of 30 seconds duration each.

The team members are not allowed to leave the court, nor is the coach allowed on the court. As soon as time-out is called, it is essential that the team members go to the sidelines quickly in order to give the coach time to make corrections and/or reassignments. Only the coach or team captain may call a time-out.

Learning Experience

Your team is playing the third game of a match. The score is 12 to 9 in your favor. Your best spiker, a poor defensive player and a weak server, has just rotated to the right back position. You wish to substitute him. What type of substitute would you put into the game, and why?

12. Coeducational play differs in player line-up, more than one hit on a side, and blocking rules.

In the coed rules, the players must line up on the court alternately: boy, girl, boy, girl. After the serve they are allowed to switch positions. If a ball is contacted more than one time on a side, it must be touched by a girl before it crosses the net. The net height is eight feet. One backcourt player may also block when there is only one male player in a front line position.

OUTCOMES

After studying this chapter, you should be able to:

1. Name the rule-governing body for open volleyball in this country and for international competition.
2. Diagram a volleyball court, showing dimensions and lines.
3. Explain how a match is won.
4. Demonstrate how the three front row players line up before the serve in order to be in proper rotation order.
5. Demonstrate how the back row players line up before the serve in relation to the front row players.
6. Explain how the ball is put into play.
7. Explain how players may shift positions after the serve, and the reason they may do this.
8. Explain why the dig or bump pass is usually used in receiving the serve.
9. Demonstrate a legal "dink" when changing the direction of the ball.
10. Describe the circumstances in which a player may extend his hands across the net.
11. Demonstrate how an off-balance spiker may cross over the centerline without constituting a foul.
12. State how many times a substitute may reenter a game and how many team substitutions are permitted in a game.
13. State the number of time-outs permitted in a game and the length of each.

4

Basic Offensive and Defensive Strategies

CONCEPT: The basic offensive strategy is designed to set the ball up and spike it over the net, while the basic defenses attempt to block the spike or establish their own attack.

The purpose of the offense is to hit the ball over the net in such a manner that the defense cannot return it. This is usually accomplished by jumping high in the air and spiking the ball over the net into the opponents' court. Two defensive players usually attempt to prevent the spike from coming over the net by blocking the ball after the spiker has hit it. The rest of the defensive players are deployed to recover the ball in the event it gets by the blockers.

1. The basic offensive alignment is the four-two, which employs four spikers and two setters.

This system employs four players, called *spikers*, whose job it is to get the ball over the net; and two players called *setters*, whose job it is to set the ball. The offensive pattern of the four-two calls for the ball to be passed close to the net in the center front of the court; for the setter to set the ball to the right or left front corners of the net; and for the spiker to hit the ball over the net (Fig. 4.1). Since the setter is always close to the net, it becomes the job of the five remaining players to pass the first ball to him. After the first ball is passed, the players at the net have specialized jobs: that is, the setter is to get to the pass and set the ball, while one of the two remaining spikers hits the ball across the net.

The five serve-receivers line up in a receiving formation that resembles an M, with the setter close to the net (Fig. 4.2A, B). When the setter is in the middle front rotation order (Fig. 4.2B), he should face his strongest spiker and position himself about ten feet from the opposite sideline. In this position the setter will have ample opportunity to deliver front sets to his strongest spiker.

A. Pass B. Set C. Spike

Photographs courtesy of Stan Troutman

Figure 4.1. Fundamental Offensive Techniques

A. Setter in His Team's Right Front Court   B. Setter in Middle Front

Figure 4.2. Serve-Receiving Formation

Photographs courtesy of Stan Troutman

1a. When the front row setter rotates to an outside position, he must switch to the center after the serve, so as to be able to set to either spiker. Because the ball is usually passed to the center of the court, the setters in the left and right front positions must move to the center front to receive the pass. This is called "switching". The "switch" is started as soon as the ball is served, and the setter can remain in this position until the ball is dead. Before the next serve, the setter must return to his original position in the rotation.

In the rotation (Fig. 4.3B), the setter in the front row is in the right front position. The spiker in the center front moves as close to the right side as possible, without overlapping the position of the setter. The remaining players line up as they did when the setter was in the middle. The next rotation moves the setter from the back row to the left front position. This time the center front spiker crowds as close to the left sideline as possible, again without overlapping the setter's position (Fig.

BASIC OFFENSIVE AND DEFENSIVE STRATEGIES 43

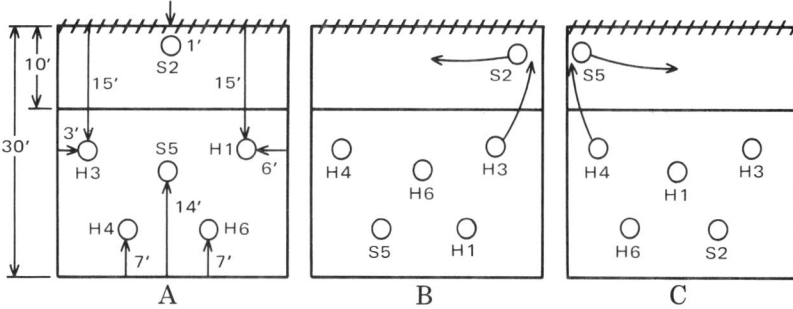

Figure 4.3. Setter Switch

4.3C). If the spiker lines up close to the setter before the serve, it is easy and natural for him to make the switch.

1b. The two setters line up diagonally opposite each other, as do the two best spikers, so that one will always be in the front row. As basic fundamentals are learned, and as skill and experience increase, you will find that the strongest spikers will become apparent. In order always to have one strong hitter at the net, a team must line up the two best spikers diagonally opposite one another, leaving the remaining two spikers also opposite. As the setter "switches" into the middle, one of the spikers must "switch" with the setter to the outside. If the best spikers are lined up so that they precede a setter in the service order, they should switch so as to hit twice from their "on-hand" or left front side (right-handed spiker). In Fig. 4.3B, spiker no. 4 who is left front, spikes from the "on-hand" side as the setter no. 2 "switches" into the center. In Fig. 4.3C, after the rotation of setter no. 2 to the back row, the other setter, no. 5, comes to the net. Spiker no. 4 now switches with the setter next to him, and therefore hits for the second time from the left front position. A left-handed spiker should line up so as to hit twice from his "on-hand," or right side.

When the setters rotate to the middle of the court, there is no need to "switch." The front spikers pull back off the net to about center court, with the left front player very near the left sideline, and the right front player crowding toward the center of the court toward the side from which the opponents are serving. The center back player is in the center of the court, even with or slightly behind the front row players in order to cover the area vacated by the setter, who is at the net. The two left and right back players stand two or three feet behind, and between the front row players (Fig. 4.3A).

Learning Experience: Four-Two Offense

Have a team of six players line up to receive the serve. Start with the setter in the center front position. The server serves easily, the receiving team passes, sets, and spikes the ball. How many passes are placed accurately enough for the setter to get under the ball? Does the setter move for every pass? Do the hitters allow the setter to set the ball, so they are always ready to spike the ball?

Rotate, so the setter "switches" in from the right front. Is there any problem in switching? Does the setter still get to the ball? Rotate again. Repeat until each player at the net knows his job thoroughly.

On the bad pass, is the ball set to the front corners? After the set, do the players "back up" their spiker? Do the players cover each other on serve reception?

1c. The setter has several options in setting the ball, depending on his skill, the effectiveness of his spikers and the reaction of the defense. Forward sets are usually delivered with greater accuracy than over-the-head or "back sets." The average setter should face his effective or "hot" spiker whenever possible, so that he can take advantage of the better percentages involved in the forward set. Hitters often compile a fantastic spiking percentage for one game, match, or tournament. The good setter takes advantages of streaks like this and sets numerous balls to them. The beginning setter should not attempt to deliver difficult sets to confuse his opposition, but should concentrate on good percentage plays.

When the serve is passed well, the skilled setter may back-set the ball over his head in order to confuse the block. The setter should watch his opponents' blocking alignment, in order to capitalize on a small or weak blocker aligned against a good spiker.

The ideal play for the advanced setter is to deliver a good set while fooling the block. This can be accomplished by the setter watching the blockers out fooling the block. This can be accomplished by the setter watching the blockers out of the corner of his eye, and trying to catch them moving or "cheating" toward one of the spikers and then delivering the ball in the opposite direction. Deception is a good goal for the setter if the accuracy of the set is not impaired.

1d. When the ball is served, everyone's job is to back up the passer. As in Fig. 4.3A, if the ball is served to the left front no. 3, the left back no. 4 moves behind no. 3 in case the ball goes back overhead. The center back covers no. 3 for the ball rebounding off to the right. If the ball is served to the right front, the right back and center back cover in the same way. If the ball is served to the center back, he is covered by the left and right back players. When the ball is served to either the left or right back players, they in turn back up each other for the missed ball that goes deep, while the center back player covers the pass that rebounds diagonally off the passer's arms rather than going forward to the center of the court. If the pass does not reach the center front position, one of the back row players must be ready to step in and set the ball to either of the front corners.

BASIC OFFENSIVE AND DEFENSIVE STRATEGIES

Figure 4.4. Backing Up the Passer

Photo courtesy of Stan Abraham

1e. After the set, all players back up the spiker to handle block rebounds. This means covering him in case the ball rebounds off the blocker's hands back into their court. If the ball is set to the left front spiker, the setter and other players move quickly in unison to a designated area. The left back comes in behind the spiker down the line from two to five feet behind him, depending upon how close the set is to the net. The center back comes in the same distance behind the spiker, and between the left back and setter. The setter completes the half circle that surrounds the spiker, by being about two to three feet from the net. The right front player pulls back off the net toward the rear of the court, and the right back moves just beyond the center of the court to the left side near the baseline; both are then ready for a ball hit deep off the block

(Fig. 4.5A). When the set is to the right front player, the coverage is exactly the same on the opposite side of the court (Fig. 4.5B). If the ball is set within 18 inches of the net against tall aggressive blockers, the back-up players should crowd very close to the spiker in anticipation of the ball being blocked straight down. Against a small or poor block, this tactic is not necessary.

Learning Experience: Four-Two Spiker Coverage

Line up a complete team on one side of the net. On the other side have a "feeder," ball chasers and a hander. Throw a ball over the net having the team pass, set, and spike. After the ball is spiked, the "feeder" moves directly in front of the spiker and throws the ball back over the net as if it were blocked back. The throws should vary from straight down off the block to deep in the back court off the blockers hands. If everyone is covering, the ball should be dug back up, reset and spiked. Repeat throwing the ball back over.

Do the players stay low to the ground, with their weight forward? Can they dig the ball high enough for the setter to get to it and set it? How many times can the offense return the ball off of the block before it hits the ground?

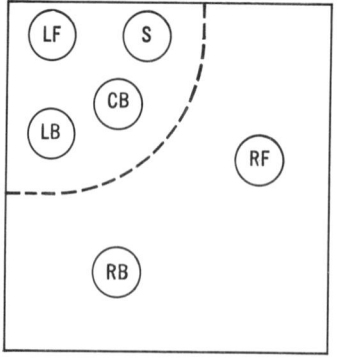 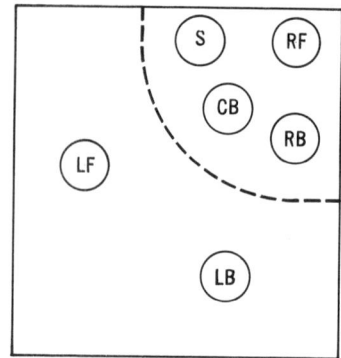

A. Left Front Spiking   B. Right Front Spiking

Figure 4.5. Covering the Spiker

1f. Common errors in executing the four-two offense can be eliminated by attention to details. Common errors in the four-two system are: 1) *The setter in the front row forgets to switch and go after the pass, regardless of where it is, and then return to the proper rotation order.* The setter must drill constantly on moving rapidly for every pass, so the spikers become more confident in the setter's ability to get the ball to them. The setter

BASIC OFFENSIVE AND DEFENSIVE STRATEGIES 47

Figure 4.6. Backing up the Spiker

Photo courtesy of Stan Abraham

Photographs courtesy of Dennis Keller

The girls in the above two photographs are utilizing a Block-It to practice backing up the spiker. This device rebounds the ball at random speeds in random directions and has proven to be an effective coaching aid.

must learn to see what position the back row setter is in, and line up opposite him before the serve. 2) *When there is a bad pass that the setter is unable to reach, no one moves to step in and set the ball.* When the ball is passed in the backcourt, or is too low to give the setter a chance to get under it, or when the ball is passed behind or in the opposite direction from which the setter is moving, the back row players must be ready to step in and set. It is easier for the back row players to set because they are already deep and facing toward the net. 3) *When the ball is badly passed, the spiker sets it to the wrong area of the net.* The ball should usually be set wide to the left or right front corner, since that is where the hitters are positioned. If the ball is set by a back row player, it should always be set diagonally crosscourt, thus giving the hitter a better angle to approach the ball. It should rarely be set to the center front position, because the setter is usually moving for the pass and is not in a good position to spike the ball.

2. Teams must be able to make quick adjustments from defense to offense, and vice versa.

When a team serves, the three front row players stay at the net to block. The team serving must anticipate a good pass, a good set, and then the spike. If the pass is not good, and the setter has trouble getting to the ball

Figure 4.7. No Block

Photo courtesy of Stan Abraham

BASIC OFFENSIVE AND DEFENSIVE STRATEGIES 49

or a back row player must step in and set the ball, the defense should be ready for a bad set. If the set is from six to ten feet back off the net, even though the spiker approaches to spike the ball, the blockers yell "NO BLOCK." With this call, the setter remains at the net and the spikers move off the net, with the remaining players assuming their serve reception positions—except that they crowd to the center of the court (Fig. 4.8A). When the ball must be hit over the net with a chest pass or bump, the defensive team calls "FREE BALL." With this call, they assume a normal serve-reception position, with the setter still at the net (Fig. 4.8B). The individual passing a free ball should "call" for it, in the same way a baseball outfielder calls for a fly ball.

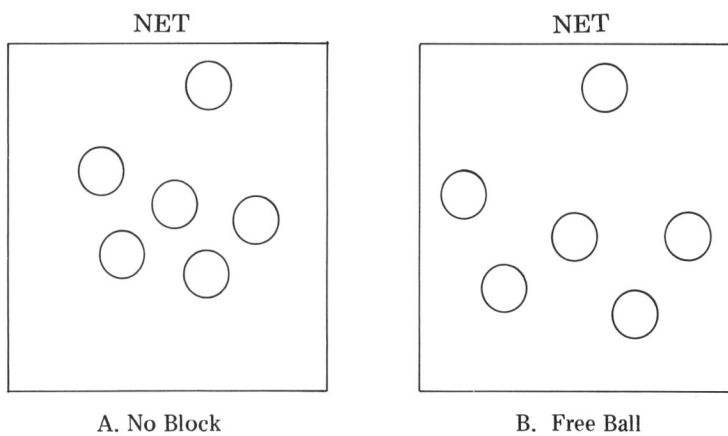

Figure 4.8. Defending Broken Plays from the Opponents' Left

The difference between the "no block" and "free ball" play is that, in the "no block," the set is good enough to be hit by the spiker in a downward angle but not sharply enough to block; whereas, in the "free ball," the ball usually travels over the net in an upward flight.

The four-two system is the basic offensive formation of volleyball. Whatever advanced systems are used, once the first pass is not perfect enough to work plays, a team must revert to the simple four-two pattern. It is essential that this pattern be understood and established before any advanced system be tried.

Learning Experience: "No Block" and "Free Ball" Situations

Line a complete team up on one side of the net. Instruct the remaining players to form two spiking lines, with a setter on the opposite side of the court. Toss the ball to the setter in various positions around the court, and instruct the setter to vary the distance of his sets from the net to either of the spikers. The defense will block the ball on a good set, call "NO" on a questionable set and "FREE" on a bad set. Can some players analyze the correct call quickly with consistency? Does this technique work better when one player is assigned to call the defensive formation? Does the defense react quickly to the call? Do all the players know the court area they are assigned to in each of the three situations?

---

3. The defense must prepare for the offensive tactics of the opponent.

The two basic defensive alignments used in competitive volleyball are called the *red* and the *white* defenses. In both defenses, every player is assigned an area of the court and is expected to allow his teammates to field balls that are out of his area of play. The zone varies according to where the ball is set and how the blockers defend against the attacking spiker.

An individual's stance (Fig. 4.9A) is the same in all defenses. The body is in a semi-crouch position, with the feet spread slightly more than shoulder width. The weight is forward and on the balls of the feet, with hands held waist high.

Teams should assume the team starting position (Fig. 4.9B) before changing into the red or white defense, so that their opponents cannot identify their defensive alignment. They should assume the same starting position until they see that the ball is going to be set. The traditional American defense has been the white alignment, while most European teams use variations of the red or white defense to meet the changing offensive tactics of their opponents.

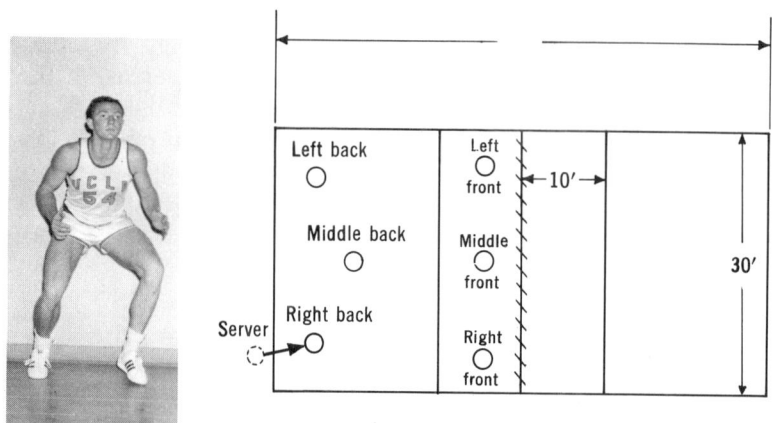

A. Individual Starting Position   B. Team Starting Position

Photo courtesy of Stan Troutman

Figure 4.9. Defensive Starting Position

BASIC OFFENSIVE AND DEFENSIVE STRATEGIES 51

The blockers in both defensive alignments should extend their arms over the net in order to contact the ball on the attacking team's side. To counteract blockers who reach over the net, opposing setters must set the ball away from the net to enable spikers to hit away from the block. Spikers can no longer merely jump up and smash the ball as hard as they can, but must rely on an assortment of spikes, drop shots, or "dinks" and off-speed hits to put the ball on the floor. This variety in the spiker's offensive arsenal has caused the emergence of the red defense, which covers many of the attacker's soft shots.

4. The red defense protects against off-speed hits.

Teams that rely on the dink shot (Fig. 4.10A) should find this defense very difficult to crack. Balls that are looped over the block are covered by a backcourt player (CB), who positions himself behind the block just inside the ten-foot line (Fig. 4.10B). Hard-driven spikes are left to his deeper teammates (LF, LB, RB), who have more time and space to react.

The right back man is responsible for spikes that are hit down his line and long balls that are hit off the block on his side of the court. His starting position is five feet in from the endline and three to five feet off the sideline. Occasionally the spiker may attempt to dink a long ball to the middle of the court. In this event, the defensive responsibility is shared between the left back and the right back. The left back (LB) should position himself in a direct line with the ball and the armswing of the spiker; he should start about five feet in from the endline and sideline. His primary responsibility is hard-driven spikes hit inside the middle

A. Dink Shot

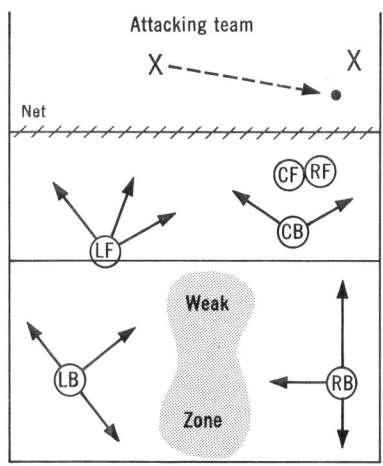

B. Red Defense

Figure 4.10. Defending Against Off-Speed Shots and Dinks

Photo courtesy of Stan Abraham

blocker. He is also responsible for dinks and off-speed spikes to the center of the court and deep balls hit over the block. The left front or off-blocker should move to a starting position on the ten-foot line, about five feet from the sideline, ready to move laterally or forward. He is the primary digger for all spikes hit inside the block and all short and medium dinks on the left side of the court. The starting positions of these four defensive players sets up a "square" formation, keeping equal distances between players on the court (Fig. 4.10B). When the ball is set toward the center of the court, the off-blocker (LF) should move closer to the near sideline while, on wide sets, he should move toward the center of the court. The remaining players also adjust with the set, so that the formation of the "square" defense is always apparent.

Learning Experience: Red Defense, Off-Blocker Position

Tape X's on the court, ten feet from the net and seven feet from the sideline on both sides of the court. When you are in the front corner and the ball is set away from you, run to the X before the spiker attacks the ball. Are you in a crouching position with your hands waist high? Is your weight distributed on the balls of your feet? Are your feet spread so you can move laterally? Can you move or dive forward rapidly to cover balls that are dinked, hit off the block or spiked softly? Can you get into position before the ball is hit? Do you move toward the sideline on an inside set, and toward the center of the court on a wide set?

The center front and right front are attempting to block the ball back into the opponent's court (Fig. 4.10B). They should not attempt to block any dink shots unless they can drive the ball sharply down into the attacker's court, since the center back man behind the block is in an excellent position to field dinks. The outside blocker should line up about three feet from the sideline. If the ball is set toward the center of the court, the block should move toward the middle of the court. The inside blocker (CF) has the primary responsibility for closing any holes in the block on a wide set, while the outside blocker (RF) has the primary responsibility to close the block on an inside set.

5. The white defense protects against hard-driven spikes.

Hard-hitting teams that spike off the top and over the block without varying their attack with dinks and off-speed shots can be stopped by this defense. Generally, blockers should stay closer to the sideline than they do in the red defense, to force the spiker to hit crosscourt (Fig. 4.12) where two or three players will have an opportunity to field the ball. When the blockers leave the line shot open on the spiker's strong side,

BASIC OFFENSIVE AND DEFENSIVE STRATEGIES 53

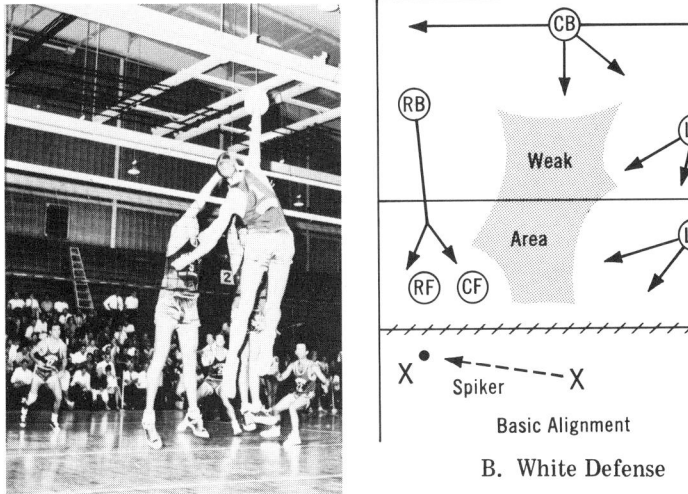

A. Spiking Over the Block   *Photo courtesy of Doctor Leonard P. Stallcup*

B. White Defense

Figure 4.11. Defending Against Spikes Hit over the Block

there is considerable pressure placed on the backcourt player defending the line (RB, Fig. 4.11B).

Number 22 in Fig. 4.13 is playing the right backcourt position in the white defense, and is responsible for covering spikes hit down the line and any dinks looped over by the block. Having studied the spiker until a split second before impact, he has ruled out the possibility of a dink and has moved close to the floor in preparation for a hard-driven spike. The initial

Photo courtesy of Stan Troutman

Figure 4.12. Blockers Forcing the Spiker to Hit Crosscourt

Figure 4.13. Anticipating the Spike

starting position for the player behind the block is ten feet in from the endline, near the sideline.

The center back man (CB, Fig. 4.11B) is responsible for balls hit off the top of the block and over the head of the left and right back men. Although he is not charged with the short dink shot, he must be ready to move forward if he sees a chance to dig a spike that gets through a space between the blockers' hands. His starting position is in a direct line behind his blockers and the attacking spiker. He is positioned just inside the endline and moves laterally in the direction the spiker hits the ball. This position is often compared to the free safetyman in football.

Learning Experience: White Defense: Center Back Player Sets A Ball Hit Off The Blockers' Hands

Stand in the center back position on the endline (CB, Fig. 4.11B), and instruct your partner to throw balls to you from the blocking positions on your side of the net. Can you set these balls 11 to 16 feet high and hit a chair placed three feet from the net and on the sideline on your side of the court? Can you cause three consecutive sets to hit the chair on the left? The chair on the right?

BASIC OFFENSIVE AND DEFENSIVE STRATEGIES

The left back defender (LB, Fig. 4.11B) is the primary crosscourt digger. By aligning himself off the left shoulder of the center blocker, he can see the ball and the spiker when contact is made. Most balls that go around the block will come to this player. He must stay low, or he will touch many balls that would otherwise go out.

The left front or off-blocker should move about eight feet away from the net, taking care not to cut off the spiking angle from the left back defender. This player is the key to the defensive positioning of the left and center back players. He must move back off the net so that the other two players can space themselves so as to form a semi-circle. Besides the hard-driven spike inside the block, many of the balls fielded will be dinks or balls hit off the block. An aggressive block will force the setter to place the ball three or four feet away from the net, so that most spikers will not be able to angle hard-driven spikes at the off-blocker.

6. The decision as to where to direct the serve will depend upon the opposing team's personnel and formation.

One of the most important choices each player has to make is where to direct his serve. Even the fastest and most deceptive serves can be passed with accuracy if they are received by a good passer. Therefore, the choice you make is a strategic one. If there are no apparent weaknesses in your opponents' fundamental passing ability, try to locate a player who is out of position. Is one player trying to cover too much territory? Is the front row back too far and open for a short serve? Is the back row too close and vulnerable for a long serve? If the setter is slow afoot, serve to a deep corner of the court; if a spiker is a weak hitter, serve to his side of the court so his chances of receiving the set are increased.

If every opponent is a good passer and in correct position, the server must recognize the weakness of the formation itself. Receiving positions that are available to serve for the four-two and six-two are diagrammed below. The six-two formations utilize three front row spikers, with the setter running in from the backcourt. This adds a great deal of flexibility to the attack.

The serve against the four-two formation (Fig. 4.14A) is placed deep and down the line, in the hope that the setter will have to travel a good distance for the pass and be unable to maneuver into position for a good set. The crosscourt serve is designed to force the setter to deliver the ball to the off-hand spiker or back-set the strong side spikers.

The serve against the six-two formation (Fig. 4.14B) can be directed either at the anticipated path of the setter, in an attempt to confuse him and the players attempting to cover him, or in the far corners, so he will have difficulty getting into position for a good set.

The serve against the middle backcourt setter (Fig. 4.14C) can be directed deep over the setter's left shoulder and between the two

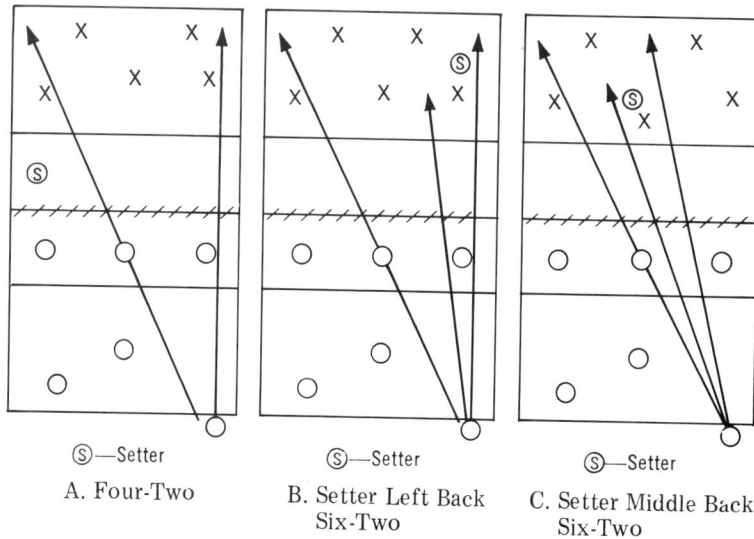

Figure 4.14. Serving Strategy

backcourt men, to confuse their receiving responsibility. Other options are to serve into the setter's path as he attempts to run around the middle front receiver, or crosscourt, so the setter will be forced to use a back set to the strong side spikers.

Learning Experience: Serving Strategy

Line a complete team up on one side of the net. Practice serving balls to all the team members until you have selected the weakest passer. Serve every ball to the weak receiver as he rotates across the front and back court. Can you force him to receive the serve on eight of ten attempts? Do you have to sacrifice the speed of your serve for accuracy? Can you force the receiver to move forward to pass the serve? Left? Right? Is there any position to which you have difficulty serving? Are his teammates attempting to cover him and create other vulnerable areas for your serve? If a team is not available, set up six chairs in a receiving formation and attempt to hit each chair with your serve.

OUTCOMES

After studying this chapter, you should be able to:

1. Explain the purpose of the four-two system.
2. Diagram the position of the players in a four-two offense and indicate

BASIC OFFENSIVE AND DEFENSIVE STRATEGIES 57

which are setters, the best two spikers and the other two spikers. Explain the reason for placing each player in that position.

3. Explain how a spiker in the center front position knows which position to switch to after the serve.
4. List the factors that determine where and how the setter may set the ball and explain how each affects his decision.
5. Diagram the position of each player when the ball is served in relation to each of the other players on the court, and explain the responsibility of each player in each of the six situations.
6. State the responsibility of every player after the ball is set. Diagram the position of the other five players if the ball is set to the left spiker and the right spiker.
7. Describe two common errors in the four-two offense and explain how they can be eliminated.
8. Diagram the position of each player on a "no block" and "free ball" play and explain the difference between them.
9. Diagram the red defense, with two blockers opposing a strong side spiker. Circle the areas of the court that are vulnerable to the spiker's attack.
10. Diagram the white defense, with two blockers opposing a strong side spiker. Circle the areas of the court that are vulnerable to the spiker's attack.
11. Briefly describe two situations in which the white and red defenses should be used.
12. Explain why the white defense was used by most teams in the United States before over-the-net blocking was adopted.
13. Describe three weaknesses to look for when selecting a player or area for your serve.
14. Discuss the weak receiving areas inherent in the four-two and six-two formations.
15. Demonstrate the correct defensive stance.

5

Advanced Skills for Power Players

CONCEPT: Advanced players improve their ability to block, dig, set, and vary their attack.

The difference between an average player and a good player is the proficiency with which he executes the basic skills, the advanced skills that he masters, and the way he executes these skills in various situations. Not only do good players execute the basic skills needed to block, recover, set up, and spike well, but they learn better techniques for doing these things, so that they can perform them in a variety of situations to improve their game.

1. Blockers can improve their game by reacting correctly in certain situations.

The following principles will help a blocker make the best use of his skills in an existing situation:

1) Block more of the line on a white defense, less on a red defense.
2) Every opposing spiker has favorite shots; learn them.
3) Signals are often exchanged between the spiker and the setter prior to the serve; close observation of the opposition's signals will often tell the blocker what type of set to expect.
4) A closer starting position prior to the spiker's approach indicates there is a play between the spiker and the setter.
5) Do not block an average spiker on a poor set.
6) Block a good spiker on a poor set.
7) Inexperienced or average spikers hit significantly more crosscourt angles than line shots from both the strong and weak sides.
8) A strong or "on-hand" spiker can hit the line shot with greater accuracy and power than a weak or "off-hand" spiker.
9) When blocking a taller player with a normal armswing or a spiker with a slow armswing, force yourself to jump later than you normally do.

ADVANCED SKILLS FOR POWER PLAYERS

10) Tired or off-balance spikers tend to dink or hit off the blocker's hands.
11) Short spikers usually have developed a good line shot.

2. Reading the spiker, presenting false weaknesses, and turning the spike in are all techniques that can improve the effectiveness of the block.

2a. A spiker's intentions can be "read" by an experienced blocker. Spikers usually attempt to avoid the block by hitting the ball crosscourt or down the line. Better blockers will know whether the normal spiker plans to hit inside or outside the block by analyzing or "reading" the spiker's approach to the set, his body alignment to the ball and—most important—his armswing. All spikers give some indication of where they plan to hit the ball, although better spikers try to conceal their intentions until the last split second or when the blockers are in mid-air. This limits the blocker's lateral movement to two or three feet in any direction.

The following guidelines will help the blocker "read" or analyze certain types of spikers:

1) Spikers with a 90-degree or straight approach to the net are in a good position to hit a line shot.
2) When the ball is set close to the sideline, it is easy for the spiker to hit the ball down the line.
3) As balls are set farther away from the net, the tendency to hit crosscourt is increased.
4) The greater the angle to the net of the approaching spiker, the greater the chance of a crosscourt spike.
5) If the ball is inside the spiker's attacking shoulder, he will probably hit the ball across his body.
6) The left shoulder often drops just prior to a crosscourt spike.
7) On a low quick set, the spiker will almost always hit the ball crosscourt.
8) If the spiker runs under the ball, expect a high flat spike or an off-speed shot.
9) A slow approach or lack of height in the spiker's jump usually indicates an off-speed attack.

Learning Experience: Reading The Spiker

Face your partner on the opposite side of the net, at the left front position. He will jump and simulate a spike without a ball. Your job is to analyze his body position and armswing, and form a block where the ball would have to be hit. Move in a sliding motion to the center, jump and block the simulated spike again; move to the right front and repeat. Do your hands form a wall in front of your opponent's spiking arm? Can you reach over the net six inches? Twelve inches? Do you jump higher on the block when you squat low before leaving the floor? Are you concentrating on your opponent's armswing and body alignment? After several trips across the net, have the spiker toss the ball to himself and spike it while you block him. If you miss the ball, can you tell the spiker at what point the ball went by your hands? Can you block eight of fifteen spikes on his side of the court?

2b. A false weakness in the block is occasionally employed to stop better spikers who like to watch the block closely. An example is the blocker who positions himself well inside the line and, in effect, issues an invitation to the spiker to hit outside his position. When the spiker starts his armswing the blocker quickly closes the unprotected area by moving his arms toward the line. The initial jump brings a blocker to his starting point; through lateral movement of his arms (Fig. 5.1B), an effective blocker can protect four to five feet of the net.

The same "false weakness" can be used to draw the spike to the middle or inside of the block. This blocking technique would be futile against beginning spikers who simply jump and hit the ball as hard as possible, regardless of where the block has formed.

2c. The outside blocker should protect the sideline by reaching over the net and placing the outside hand between the ball and the out-of-bounds area, to turn the ball into the opponent's court. Fig. 5.3 illustrates this.

A. Initial Position   B. Lateral Movement

Figure 5.1. Closing the Unprotected Zone

Photographs courtesy of Stan Troutman

ADVANCED SKILLS FOR POWER PLAYERS

This prevents the ball from being wiped off the blocker's hands into the stands, where the backcourt players cannot pursue it. (Fig. 5.4).

Learning Experience: Turning The Spike In

Have a spiker stand on a chair four feet away from the net on the opposite side of the court, with an ample number of volleyballs. Assume the outside blocker's position three feet from the sideline and one foot from the net. When the spiker hits the balls over the net down your sideline, attempt to block the ball into the middle of his court. Raise your arms to a 45° angle and move them from the sideline to the center of the court. Can you turn eight out of ten spikes into the center of his court? Can you block the balls to the floor within five feet of the net on his court? Continue the same drill, using a setter and a spiker. When you can turn eight out of ten spikes in successfully, add a middle blocker and instruct the spiker to hit crosscourt as well as down the line.

---

3. The diving recovery, shoulder roll, overhand pass, and one-arm dig are skills that will enable a player to handle hard-to-reach balls.

Mastery of the dive and rolls can increase an individual's court coverage from 25 to 75 percent. The learning progression for these skills can be started on the gym floor without the use of a ball. Beginners should put

Figure 5.2. The Rolling Dig

Photo courtesy of Stan Abraham

on kneepads and a sweatsuit until the fundamental techniques are mastered.

3a. A dive to reach balls far away from you can be cushioned by the hands and a slide. Assume a crouched position and jump forward. Raise your legs and feet higher than your waist and keep your back arched and your head up. After contacting the ball, extend your arms at a 45° angle and push against the floor with your hands to cushion the impact of the fall (Fig. 5.5). Allow your body to spend its momentum by sliding along the floor on your chest and stomach. If you dive correctly, the force will usually be spent while sliding over a large area. If you start from an erect position or do not jump, sliding will be difficult and the force will usually be absorbed by the body in one jolting bounce.

Learning Experience: The Diving Recovery

Assume a crouched position ten feet from a feeder, who will lob the ball somewhere in front of you. Attempt to pass the ball 15 feet in the air and back into the feeder's hands. Use the one-arm dig shown in Figure 5.6 or the backhand recovery pass shown in Figure 5.5. After passing the ball, spread your hands and extend the arms to the

Figure 5.3. Turning the Spike In
*Photo courtesy of
Barry Schreiber*

Figure 5.4. Wiping Off the Blocker
*Photo courtesy of
Stan Abraham*

ADVANCED SKILLS FOR POWER PLAYERS 63

Photographs courtesy of Stan Troutman

Figure 5.5. Cushioning the Dive

floor to cushion the fall (Fig. 5.5). Can you see your hand contact the ball? Do you remember to start low? Does the backhand recovery allow you to land more easily than the one-arm dig? Which pass can you control the best?

Photographs courtesy of Stan Troutman

Figure 5.6. The Diving Recovery

3b. The shoulder roll enables the defensive player to gain his feet immediately after going to the floor to dig a ball (Fig. 5.7). The shoulder roll moving to your left is the most difficult to master, since most players do not move to this side as well. Start in a squatting position and take a wide step to the side with your left leg. Your left ankle rotates outward, left toe pointing in the direction from which the stride step began. Your arms are fully extended in front of your body and the center of your body is directly behind the ball. As your body lowers to a sitting position, the ball is contacted just before your buttocks hit the floor. After contact, your body continues to roll, so that first your entire upper back and then your right shoulder come in contact with the floor. Your legs remain bent, and your body continues to roll over your right shoulder, with your hands propelling your body to an upright position.

Learning Experience: Dig And Shoulder Roll

Start low to the ground, ready to dig. Your partner stands ten feet away and tosses the ball right or left, just out of your reach. Take a lateral step, lean to the side and dig the ball, use a shoulder roll to regain your feet and prepare to recover the next ball. Can you dig balls tossed to the left as well as the right? Instruct your partner to throw the majority of balls to your weak side. Can you set the balls directly over your partner's head? Instruct your partner to vary the height of the ball, so that you can practice digging using both the overhand and forearm pass.

Once the dives and rolls have been learned, game-condition drills should be used to practice these techniques.

Learning Experience: Defensive Play

A partner stands 20 feet away from the defensive player or "digger" and hits balls just within the digger's reach (Fig. 5.8A). After passing and returning to his feet, the digger quickly reacts to the next hit. The drill is more realistic if balls are hit over the net. The spiker stands on a table or ladder and delivers a wide assortment of off-speed and hard-driven balls to two defenders (Fig. 5.8B). The player who does not dig the ball must run under the pass and set the ball, then hustle back into position for the next hit. The digger rolls to his feet and spikes the set.

Many times during the course of a game, easy balls played with the forearms could have been passed with greater accuracy had the player maneuvered under the ball to use a low overhand pass (Fig. 5.9). The

ADVANCED SKILLS FOR POWER PLAYERS 65

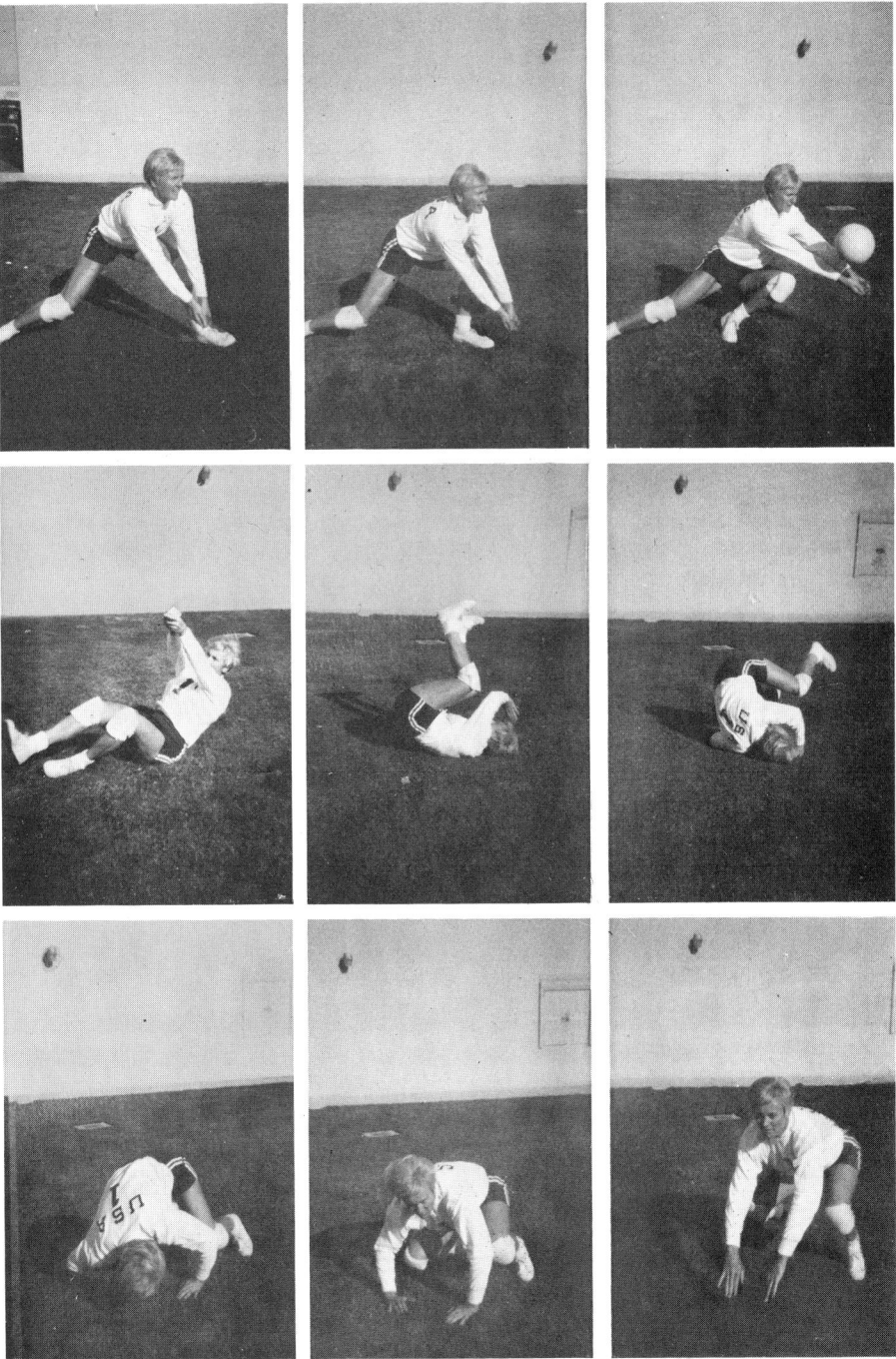

Figure 5.7. Dig and Shoulder Roll

A. Digging Drill   B. Dig, Set and Spike

Figure 5.8. Defensive Play

Photographs courtesy of Stan Troutman

Figure 5.9. Low Overhand Pass

opportunity usually occurs on dinked balls or on balls that have rebounded off the block. A good passer will often use a full squat in order to place his hands under the ball.

Learning Experience: Low Overhand Pass

Assume a low squatting position and use the overhand pass to recover low balls that your partner tosses to you. Can you set the ball to him? After you set the ball, can you regain your feet quickly for the next play? Concentrate on getting the shoulders under the ball, and contacting the ball with your fingers in front of your eyes. Try to increase your range of coverage by setting balls thrown to the left and right of you. When you are forced to move laterally, can you pivot on your inside foot in order to face your partner as you pass the ball?

3c. **The one-arm dig is a recovery play, and should not be used if the ball can be reached with the forearm or overhand pass.** In both the standing and diving positions, the ball is usually bounced off one forearm just above the wrist (Fig. 5.10A).

Photo courtesy of Dr. Leonard B. Stallcup

A. One-Arm Dig   B. Net Recovery

Figure 5.10. Recovery Plays

Learning Experience: Net Recovery

Instruct a teammate to spike balls into the top, middle, and bottom of the net; attempt to recover the spikes using the forearm pass or one-arm dig. Alternate, setting the ball as if it were the second contact and bump it over the net as if it were the third contact. Crouch low and wait until the ball is well clear of the net just before playing it.

4. A back set to the spiker behind the setter can deceive opposing blockers.

The body position for the back set is identical to that used for the front set. The setter positions himself with his side facing the net, feet firmly planted on the floor, knees bent and hands up. The pass will travel across the center of the setter's body and the ball will be contacted above and in front of the eyes, as in the front set. The setter arches his back and keeps his elbows at shoulder height. The ball is released by flicking the fingertips as the arms and knees move upward. Setters should be capable of delivering the ball in either direction from the same position, just as baseball pitchers use the same delivery to throw curves and fast balls.

Learning Experience: The Back Set

Start with three people spaced ten feet apart and three feet away from the net. The outside player, no. 1, starts with the ball and passes it to the middle player, no. 2. The middle player back sets the ball to player no. 3, then turns around and faces him. Player no. 3 passes the ball back to the middle, who again back sets it to no. 1, and turns around to face him. Can you keep the ball moving in this manner until you have gone through the drill ten times?

Opposing blockers are constantly looking for tip-offs in the setter's form, so they can get a jump on the set. Experienced blockers expect the setter to arch his back when setting over his head, and to keep his back relatively straight when setting forward. Good setters are capable of giving blockers false clues, by faking in the wrong direction before setting the ball.

5. Four basic play sets enable the offense to vary their attack.

All play sets remain in the air for a shorter period of time than a normal

Photo courtesy of Stan Troutman
Figure 5.11. The Back Set

set, and require great coordination between the setter and spiker. Greater player satisfaction, improved team efficiency and increased spectator interest is developed through the use of well-executed play sets. The spiker or setter may call for a play set at any time during the course of the game, either before or after the serve. Play sets are automatically called off if there is a bad pass; otherwise, the spiker or spikers are totally committed to the play. The setter makes the final decision whether to deliver the play set or set a normal ball to another spiker. There should always be one spiker who is expecting a normal set, in case the opposing blockers have anticipated the play.

For purposes of simplicity, the play sets are numbered one through four.

The most exciting offensive play in volleyball is a well-executed spike of an extremely low set placed only inches above the net (Fig. 5.12). This play was popularized among athletes and spectators by the touring Japanese National Men's and Women's teams shortly after the 1964 Olympic Games. It has been used in international competition for several years, but it was perfected by the Japanese to defeat the block of their taller opponents by utilizing split-second timing between spiker and setter. The spiker moves to within a few feet of the setter while he is moving into position to receive the pass. The instant the spiker sees the setter in position to receive the pass, he gathers to jump, and is in the air before the setter touches the ball. He should be at the top of his jump just as the ball is clearing the tape (Fig. 5.12). If the blocker jumps with the spiker, the

Photo courtesy of Stan Troutman

Figure 5.12. The "One-Set"

Photo courtesy of Stan Abraham

Figure 5.13. The "Two-Set"

setter should set to another player; if the blocker does not jump, the spiker receives an easy chance to put the ball on the floor.

The *one-set* is also known as the *Japanese set;* the ball is set less than one foot above the net and is contacted by the setter as the spiker jumps in the air.

The *two-set* travels two to three feet above the net. The two-set does not require the same split-second timing as the Japanese set, and can be learned by any good spiker. Because of the extra height on the set, the spiker usually has at least one blocker defending against him. Although the approach is nearly completed before the setter touches the ball, the spiker does not jump until the setter contacts the ball (Fig. 5.13).

The *three-set* travels one to three feet above the net (normal height), and is placed seven to eight feet from either sideline. The three-set is delivered between the outside and middle blockers, in an attempt to create a space between the blockers. Since the ball is not set close to the sideline, the outside blocker is usually left out of position, with the ball being hit before the block forms.

Figure 5.14. The "Three-Set" *Photo courtesy of Jim Koski, UCLA Daily Bruin*

The "shoot," or *four-set,* is placed a few feet from the sideline. The four- or shoot-set is delivered low and fast to the outside spiker. The ball should not reach a height of more than five to six feet above the net. The play is extremely difficult for the middle blocker to cover when the ball covers a distance of 15 to 20 feet from the setter to the spiker. Unless the setter gives the play away, the middle blocker will invariably be late on the block, leaving the crosscourt area open for a hard-driven spike.

ADVANCED SKILLS FOR POWER PLAYERS

Learning Experience: Play Sets

Form three spiking lines on the left, middle, and right sides of the court. Stand close to the net, about four feet to the right of the center spiker. The center spiker will pass the ball to you, and all three spikers will approach the net for the set. Once the pass is in the air, the strong side spiker may call "THREE" or "FOUR," while the middle spiker may call "ONE" or "TWO." The weak side spiker will always expect a normal play set. Can you successfully react to a spiker's call? If the spiker does not call for a play, deliver a normal set to him. Continue the same drill with a middle blocker defending against the attack. Can the blocker anticipate where you are going to set the ball? Does the middle blocker ever reach the strong side spiker on a four-set?

In the two-hitter system, the jump set is used most effectively by the tall setter who can react with split-second timing to the opposing block. If the blocker does not jump with the setter, the setter spikes the ball; if the blocker does jump, he sets the ball and creates a one-on-one blocking situation. The jump set can be utilized by the advanced setter on any of the above play sets or a normal set.

Number 43 in Fig. 5.15 is in excellent position to spike the ball inches from the setter's fingertips. If the middle blocker jumps with the setter, the ball can be set to the other spiker, preferably on a low trajectory (four-set) to leave the middle blocker out of the play. This play takes a

Figure 5.15. Jump "One-Set" *Photo courtesy of Stan Troutman*

tremendous amount of coordination between spiker and setter, and is rarely used due to its high degree of difficulty.

6. Spiking ability improves by hitting over the block, increasing the force of the hit, developing good peripheral vision to observe blockers and learning to direct the ball with greater accuracy.

6a. The spiker who delivers a spiked ball over his opponent's block will experience a great deal of success. This will happen because most defensive alignments are built on the premise that the block is going to prevent or slow up hard-driven spikes from the area directly behind the block; therefore this area is usually unprotected. Tall spikers should have the ball set high and close to the net, to enable them to spike over the block (Fig. 5.16).

Figure 5.16. Spiking over the Block *Photo courtesy of Stan Abraham*

Learning Experiences: Spiking Over The Block

Position two blockers in the opposite court and instruct your teammate to set the ball high and close to the net. Can you spike over your opponents, or do they block the ball? Practice this until you can hit a high flat spike off the top of their fingertips three out of five times.

6b. The force of a spiked ball can be increased by arching the back and bending the knees at more than a 90-degree angle just prior to contact (Fig. 5.17B). At contact, the stomach and hip flexors contract vigorously as the upper trunk and legs snap forward from the waist. Spikers of only average jumping ability should not use this technique, since it can lower the vertical jump by two or three inches. Exceptional jumpers usually benefit from an increase in power, at the expense of a few inches in jumping height. The normal amount of arch and knee flexion is also shown in Fig. 5.17A.

A. Normal Technique   B. Power Technique

Figure 5.17. Power Spiking

Photographs courtesy of Stan Troutman

6c. Some hitters have good peripheral vision, and can see the hands of the defenders forming the block while leaping high in the air to spike the ball. Regardless of their approach to the set, they are capable of spiking the ball crosscourt or down the line by rotating their forearm and wrist inward or outward (Fig. 5.18).

The ability to see the block can be developed by having two blockers move their hands either to the left or right just prior to the spiker contacting the ball. The spiker will become aware of the blockers and learn to direct his spikes with greater accuracy. A coach standing behind the spiker can easily signal the blockers to pull their hands left or right or to leave a hole in the middle of the block. If the spiker can successfully direct the ball through a hole in the block it will seldom be fielded or

A. Crosscourt Turn   B. Line Turn

Figure 5.18. Turning the Spike

Photographs courtesy of Stan Troutman

"dug," since defensive alignments are built around the premise that the front row defenders can usually present a solid wall of hands to the spiker.

Learning Experience: Watching The Block

Following the steps presented in the previous section, spike against a moving block. Can you see the block while you are spiking? Do you see the holes in the block? Can you see the individual hands forming the block? Attempt to hit the ball off one of the defender's hands without getting blocked.

7. **The dink and off-speed spike can catch the defense off guard.**

The dink shot is most effective on a good set, when the defense is expecting a hard-driven spike. The spiker swings rapidly at the ball, leading with his elbow, extending his arm and contacting the ball with his fingertips. Contact is made as high above the net as possible, with the wrist held fairly stiff (Fig. 5.19), in comparison to the vigorous wrist snap used in the spike. When the ball is not contacted high above the net, the opposition will usually block the shot (Fig. 5.20).

ADVANCED SKILLS FOR POWER PLAYERS

A. Contact   B. Follow-Through

Figure 5.19. Dinking over the Block

Photographs courtesy of Stan Troutman

Learning Experience: Dinking

Have two blockers stand on a table next to the net. Dink a set over the blockers' hands and to the floor a few feet behind them. Alternate dinks with hard-driven spikes. Can the blockers "read" the dink shot by your approach? Remove the table and continue practicing against an aggressive block. Instruct the blockers to yell "DINK" just before contact, when they do not think you will deliver a hard-driven spike. When the blockers cannot guess correctly on more than five of ten attempts, you are on your way to mastering the technique. Direct your dink shots deep and down the line, and short to the middle front as well as just behind the blockers. Place towels in these three areas and attempt to hit the towels on seven of ten attempts.

The off-speed spike is harder for the defense to read than the dink, because the spiker contacts the ball with his open hand rather than his fingertips. It is also harder to control and has not been perfected by many players in this country. If the spiker can use relatively the same approach and armswing in delivering a soft shot as a hard-driven spike, the defense will find the ball losing momentum and landing in front of them as they are braced for the "hard kill." It is most effective when used as a change-of-pace shot and directed toward a definite weakness in the

A. Low Contact   B. Blocked Ball

Figure 5.20. Dinking Too Low

Photographs courtesy of Stan Troutman

defense—whether it be an individual or an open area of the court. The East German team uses the soft spike very effectively by looping the ball over the end blocker and deep down the line against the white defense.

OUTCOMES

After studying this chapter, you should be able to:

1. Describe two situations in which any spiker is likely to hit the ball crosscourt.
2. List four guidelines to help a blocker determine where the opposing spiker intends to place his attack.
3. Define the term "false weakness" and demonstrate how it can be utilized to block an opposing spiker.
4. Demonstrate an approach to the net that would indicate a line shot by the spiker.
5. Describe and demonstrate how an outside blocker "turns the spike in."
6. Demonstrate the front dive, shoulder roll, and low overhand pass.
7. Pass and set several balls, using diving and rolling recoveries.
8. Demonstrate the one-arm dig by recovering balls hit into the net.
9. Demonstrate how to set the ball forward and backward using the same body and arm motion.
10. Demonstrate the four play sets and explain their purposes.
11. Jump high in the air as if to spike a pass; at the last second, "shoot" the ball to a corner spiker.
12. Demonstrate the effectiveness of a high flat spike against two blockers who are taller than you.

ADVANCED SKILLS FOR POWER PLAYERS

13. Describe and demonstrate the technique used to increase the force of a spiked ball.
14. Demonstrate how the spike is directed by a rotation of the wrist.
15. Approach the net at a 45° angle and spike the ball down the line.
16. Approach the net at a 90° angle and spike the ball crosscourt.
17. Demonstrate a dink shot.
18. Describe where the dink shot should be placed against the red and white defense.
19. Demonstrate an off-speed spike and explain its use.

6

Preparation for Power Volleyball Competition

CONCEPT: A planned program of physical conditioning, skill development, and team play is necessary for successful participation in power volleyball.

Good volleyball players and teams don't just happen; they are developed by hard work and practice. Not only must players perfect their individual skills, but they must maintain top physical condition and learn to work with their teammates. It is the combination of these three factors that produces success and enjoyment in the game.

1. Physical conditioning, necessary for top performance, can be developed by specific exercises and volleyball drills.

Volleyball was originally designed for middle-aged businessmen who lobbed or volleyed the ball back and forth over the net. People who should not overexert themselves still participate in this original interpretation of the game.

The faster-moving version of the game is rapidly gaining popularity, not only for the recreational value involved, but also for the maintenance or development of physical fitness. Two-man or mixed-doubles volleyball is quite popular among the college population, since a maximum amount of exercise can be obtained in a minimum amount of time.

Adept players may seek stiffer competition by joining organized teams or entering doubles tournaments. In many instances, they find that their present physical levels are no longer adequate and that an increase in endurance and vertical jumping height is desired.

Muscular endurance is developed by working tired muscles and by weight training—using a small amount of weight, with many repetitions. The spiker who contacts the ball 30 inches above the net during warm-ups and only 20 inches above the net during the fifth game is an example of a good jumper with poor endurance.

Beginning players and national champions would increase their effectiveness if they significantly improved the height of their vertical jump while blocking and spiking (Fig. 6.1). Due to over-the-net blocking, superior jumping ability is a prerequisite to becoming an outstanding blocker.

Figure 6.1 Spiking High *Photo courtesy of Stan Troutman*

The quadriceps (knee extensors), gluteus maximus (buttocks), gastrocnemius and soleus (or calf) all contribute to performance in the vertical jump. The quadriceps supply most of the strength, with the contribution of the gluteus maximus increasing as the jumping angle between the calf and upper leg moves between 75° to 90°. Normally, smaller players will be able to jump higher if they squat close to 90°, while tall players tend to be more efficient at a lesser angle. When a player uses the correct jumping angle, the calf muscles act primarily as a positioner for the jump.

Learning Experience: Standing Vertical Jump

Cover your fingertips with chalk. Stand with your toes against the wall, feet flat on the floor. Reach as high as you can with both arms and touch the wall. Without taking a step, squat and jump to your maximum height and touch the wall above your mark. Measure the distance between the chalk marks with a yardstick to find the height of your standing vertical jump. Can you jump 24 inches or more? Would you like to increase your jump? Take the test again, using a one-quarter, one-half, three-quarter and full squat. Which jumping angle gives you the greatest height?

Pre-season and post-practice weight training will increase the height of the vertical jump significantly. The most effective method of increasing leg strength is to squat with weights that can be lifted from one to six times with a maximum effort. Weight training should be carried out through the full range of motion required during blocking and spiking. As the muscles grow stronger and the vertical jump increases weight must be increased to keep the muscles responding to the limit of their present ability.

A difficult exercise that simulates the jump in actual competition is a squat and jump performed with a barbell weighting up to 50 percent of the body weight, held on the back and shoulders. This maneuver is specific to the cells and functional elements within the muscle fibers that are actually used in the jump, and hence makes them stronger. Foam padding or towels should be wrapped around the bar, and the back should be as straight as possible, with the chest held high.

One daily repetition of 50 squats with 50 percent of your body weight will develop the leg endurance necessary to squat low in the proper defensive position and sustain a good jump during a long match. If correct technique can be maintained, the squats should be performed rapidly to increase the speed of contraction of the faster muscle fibers.

Learning Experience: Conditioning

Develop a simple conditioning program (two to four exercises) designed to improve your leg power and endurance. Participate in this program for a number of weeks. Do you notice any improvement in your jumping ability? In your ability to play the game longer without fatigue?

Physical training should be emphasized at the beginning of practice, especially in the preparatory stage of the season. *The selection, intensity and duration of the recommended exercises should depend on your aspirations and present physical condition.* In order to warm up before using intense exercises, jog, walk, and run a few laps. Intersperse periods of vertical jumping on the laps after you are warm. To avoid the monotony of running around a track or gym floor and to build leg strength, run over hilly areas and up steps. Include back, hamstring, and groin-stretching exercises with squats, arm circles, sit-ups and finger push-ups at each workout. A series of 70-yard windsprints from a jogging start with 30 second intervals is recommended to develop anaerobic capacity. Next, zigzag a 25-foot length of elastic to form a six- to 18-jump obstacle course. The elastic can be raised from two to four feet in height. Begin the exercise by simply jumping over each barrier once, then jump over and back and over again. Only your imagination will limit the various combinations that can be used. If practice is held in a gym, run to each basket and attempt to touch the rim five times before moving to the next basket. Select a partner of the same height as yourself and stand on opposite sides of the net. At five-foot intervals, jump and clap your partner's hands. Try to clap hands two and three times on the same jump.

There are several drills which combine conditioning and fundamental techniques. Some drills are done individually, and some with partners.

Learning Experiences: Conditioning and Fundamental Techniques Combined

Set chest passes to yourself for one minute, then switch to bump passes for the next minute. Sit down and pass a ball high above your head, jump up and set it to yourself, run under the ball, sit down and pass it again. Repeat for one minute, without letting the ball touch the floor. Alternate setting to yourself while squatting and standing. Select a partner, face each other and lay flat on your stomachs five to ten feet apart. Arch your backs and pass the ball back and forth. Sit up and continue passing the ball, roll backwards or sidewards to pass errant balls, turn and sit at 45-degree angles to one another, and continue the drill. Spike 20 balls in a row as quickly as possible, rest one minute and hit 15 more. Dig 30 spikes or dinks in a row. Simulate a block at the net, and after the jump run back into spiking position and hit a set ball. Repeat this procedure as quickly as possible.

---

2. The technical performance of volleyball skills can be improved by using a variety of drills.

The individual skills presented in Chapter 2 must be thoroughly developed if one is to improve his game. The only way this can be accomplished is through practicing them in a variety of situations. The following learning experiences can contribute to your further improvement.

3. Preparation for competitive volleyball involves physical, technical, and tactical training.

As in most sports, a season must be preplanned to be successful. The volleyball season is divided into preparatory and competitive stages. In the preparatory stage, players engage in competition for physical and technical training and do not require the special attention to the tactical details necessary in the competitive period.

Learning Experiences: Passing

1. Learning experiences utilizing a wall (use one ball per person):
   a) Overhand passes and bump passes can be practiced by having the individual stand at various distances from the wall and pass the ball to certain designated heights.
   b) For the more experienced player, more restrictions are added to increase the degree of difficulty. For example, allow the movement of only one foot while passing, and require the ball to strike inside a definite marked area on the wall.
2. Learning experiences using basketball facilities:
   a) Stand inside a marked area, i.e., a basketball free-throw circle or lane. Pass the ball the height of the basket, using the over-hand pass or bump.
   b) Combine the two skills, first overhand passing the ball in the air, then bumping.
   c) Attempt to pass the ball through the basket from the free-throw line.
3. Partner drills that can be incorporated and varied to maintain and motivate interest:
   a) Start by tossing the ball easily into the air to a partner, who overhand passes it back. Catch and retoss the ball each time, for control. Do the same drill, only bump the ball in return.
   b) Next, overhand pass the ball back and forth to each other continually. Now bump the ball back and forth. Change and vary the distance between partners, and the height of the passes.
   c) Pass the ball over the net, stressing height.
   d) One-on-one serving and overhand passing or bumping is not only a good drill for passing but also stresses serve control.

Additional Learning Experiences To Develop Setting Techniques

1. Partners stand parallel to the net, and practice setting the ball back and forth to a height of about 12 feet. Rotate, so that each group of partners can practice next to the net.
2. Setter stands at the net. Partner stands 10 feet from the net at the sideline, and tosses the ball to the setter. Setter practices setting the ball high to the outside front corner of the net.
3. Setter stands about 8 to 10 feet from the net, in the center of the court. Partner again stands behind the setter and tosses the ball to him. The setter should learn to let the ball pass in front of his body, and to partially face the net to set the ball.

4. *Setter stands at the net. Partner stands at the net, near the sideline, with a ball. The ball is tossed high into the air, about mid-court. The setter runs back off the net, passing the ball so that it is in the center of his body; he faces toward the net at an angle to set the ball.*

Additional Learning Experiences For Developing Skill In Spiking

1. *Line spikers up in a line on the on-hand side. Work on controlling the hit by aiming at objects such as a chair on the court. Work on crosscourt, down-the-line and cut-back shots for accuracy and speed.*
2. *Work on these same shots from the off-hand side.*
3. *To practice correct body positioning, start with a spiker standing at the net, at about center court. A partner tosses about 10 to 20 balls into the air in rapid succession. The tosses should be varied, so as to force the spiker to move right and left of center, in order to position his body behind the ball, keeping the ball in front of his right shoulder. As soon as the spiker jumps and hits the ball, another one is tossed. (This is also an excellent conditioning drill.)*
4. *Form a spiking line, and have one blocker at the net. Hit from both on- and off-hand sides against this blocker.*
5. *Add another blocker. Start with a spiking line on the on-hand side. Practice hitting the ball around the blockers or off the blockers' hands. Do the same from the off-hand side.*
6. *To drill on spiking deep sets that are far away from the net, have a person stand about 7 or 10 feet from the net and toss the ball straight up into the air. Have the spiker jump and hit these sets, with an upward motion on the back of the ball and an exaggerated wrist snap to produce the maximum overspin on the ball that makes it drop into the opponent's court. Two defensive players can be in the opposite court; these players dig the spike, set the ball from the dig and return it easily over the net.*
7. *Since the spiker's job is to be ready to approach the net to hit the ball, he must learn to back off the net quickly after a spike, so as to be ready for the next set. Have a spiker start with a ball in the spiking position. A setter stands at the net, and a third person stands center court with about 8 to 10 balls, ready to pass. The spiker passes the first ball to the setter and, after the set, approaches and spikes the ball. As the ball is spiked, the person standing center court passes a second ball to the setter. Once the spiker hits the floor after the spike, he must run back off the net*

to be ready to approach again for the second spike. This should be repeated, until the spiker has approached, hit, and backed off the net as many times as the ball is passed.

Additional Learning Experiences To Practice Techniques Of Blocking

Both individual and partner blocking drills should be practiced, coordinating your movement to the opposing spiker, timing your jump and setting your body position in relation to your blocking partner.

1. Have three players stand on chairs at the net, on both sidelines and at the middle of the court. They each hold a ball above and about six inches to a foot from the net. The blocker starts on the opposite side of the net, at the left front position, and jumps, trying to touch the ball in all three positions. The blocker may go through once, twice, or as many times as desired; then another blocker repeats the drill. The players holding the ball, after once through, may move the ball right or left to force the blocker to reach laterally for it.
2. For a good partner blocking drill, start with three blockers on one side of the net, in the left, center and right front positions. Three players stand opposite the blockers on the other side of the net, the player in the right front starting with a ball. The ball is tossed high into the air, simulating a set, to each of the players—from right front to center, to left, back to center, to right, etc. The blockers move in relation to the ball toss, trying to get a two-man block on the set. The outside player positions the block, and the middle player moves right or left to this outside man to form the block. When the set is in the center of the court, the middle man blocks the power hit, and the two outside blockers move toward him. Blockers rotate, so as to move from each position.
3. For a team blocking drill, use two spiking lines, with a setter on one side. Three blockers line up on the other side of the net, and move to block the ball where it is set. A middle spiking line can also be added. Backcourt players can be added on the blockers' side, so that a full defensive team can practice.

Training problems should be worked out together throughout the year. Practical experience shows that the results are unsatisfactory when training problems are solved separately. For instance, if at first a team takes up general physical training, then fundamental techniques, and

Month	Training Stage	Physical Training	Technical Training	Tactical Training
First	Preparatory	65%	30%	5%
Second	Preparatory	60%	30%	10%
Third	Preparatory	40%	40%	20%
Fourth	Competitive	30%	40%	30%
Fifth	Special training cycle for playoffs if successful			

Figure 6.2. Monthly Training Guide

finally offensive and defensive tactics, they are less successful. But when physical, technical, and tactical training are included in each practice session, it proves to be quite another matter. Some volleyball teams win tournaments at the beginning of the season, but their attainments at the height of the season decline. Research might prove that the athletes had completed a great amount of physical conditioning during the preparatory stage and had ignored this training phase during the competitive stage. For some time the level of the athletes' strength and endurance remained high, and therefore the results were also high. But gradually, in view of the absence of exercise for strength development, strength decreased and so did their performance.

Before a very important match or tournament, it is beneficial to hold practices in the form of a competitive cycle. The practice sessions, rest days and limbering up should closely coincide with the activity that will take place at the competition.

The athlete should accumulate a large reserve of knowledge in order to train effectively. To be specific, every athlete must know the *what* and *why* of all he does. A clear and precise understanding and awareness of the problems in training not only ensure a more successful mastery of volleyball techniques and tactics, but contribute to the effective development of power and endurance.

Learning Experience: Practice Schedule

Outline a two-hour team training schedule for volleyball practice to be held during the first month of the season and the last month of the season. How do the two differ?

OUTCOMES

After studying this chapter, you should be able to:

1. Explain the difference between strength and endurance.
2. Explain why a high vertical jump is important to the spiker.

3. Describe the factors that determine the height of an individual's jump.
4. Explain the difference between weight training for strength and weight training for endurance. Demonstrate two exercises designed to develop vertical jumping height.
5. Demonstrate six volleyball drills that combine conditioning and fundamental techniques.
6. Explain the major differences between the early preparatory and competitive stages of the volleyball season.
7. Explain why physical training should be included in every practice session throughout the year.

7

Where to Play

CONCEPT: Opportunities for participation in volleyball are available formally and informally.

1. Volleyball courts are usually found at YMCA's, schools, colleges, fraternities, playgrounds, parks, public beaches and resort areas.

Most YMCA's and public facilities schedule volleyball at particular time periods during the week. The YMCA's generally reserve a lunch hour for the businessman and a weeknight for men's open volleyball. Friday night volleyball may be part of a family program, with mixed groups participating. Recreation departments and many school systems reserve gymnasiums for volleyball one evening a week.

College intramural departments offer six-man, six-women, and coeducational volleyball in their programs, with many including doubles and mixed doubles.

2. In 1969 the National Association of Intercollegiate Athletics (NAIA) adopted volleyball as an official NAIA championship event and held its first tournament at George Williams College in Chicago.

In 1970 the National Collegiate Athletic Association (NCAA) and Division of Girls and Women's Sports held national championships. In 1971 the Association for Intercollegiate Athletics for Women (AIAW) was formed by the DGWS to provide leadership for women's intercollegiate athletic programs and to conduct all championship events *which* were formerly conducted by the DGWS. The first AIAW Junior College/Community College Championship was held at Miami Dade Community College in 1973. In 1974 the National Junior College Athletic Association (NJCAA) joined the bandwagon and held its first volleyball championship at Schoolcraft College in Livonia, Michigan. Thus, all national collegiate sports governing bodies conduct championship events in volleyball.

3. The United States Volleyball Association is the sanctioning association for formal open volleyball competition in America.

Over 20 organizations sponsoring volleyball at all levels of skill are affiliated with the USVBA. Each of the 19 regions of the USVBA is administered by a regional representative who promotes volleyball in his area. There are three levels of tournaments held within some of the stronger regions, with AA signifying the highest grade of competition. YMCA's, colleges, Armed Forces, athletic clubs, schools, playgrounds, and private teams compete in these open tournaments, which are traditionally held on Saturdays from early January to late April. In May, the teams with the strongest tournament standings in the region are approved by the regional representative to compete at the USVBA National Tournament, which determines the champions of the Men's, Women's, Senior Men's and Collegiate Divisions. The YMCA finishing highest in the Men's Division is recognized as the national YMCA champion.

Learning Experience: AA Volleyball

Evaluate competitive volleyball in your area by watching AA competition. Write to your USVBA *regional representative and request a season schedule. His address is usually known by your volleyball instructor or* YMCA *physical director, and can be found in the* Official Volleyball Rules and Reference Guide *published by the* USVBA. *It can be obtained by sending $2.00 to:* USVBA *Printer, Box 109, Berne, Ind. 46711.*

As you are exposed to the power game played by varsity athletes, you will find you are not satisfied to return to the pat-a-cake rendition of volleyball, and will seek to experience the slashing, spiking, and frantic dives to the hardwood that make the game of power volleyball so fascinating.

OUTCOMES

After reading this chapter, you should be able to:

1. List the organizations in your area that offer volleyball facilities for public or private use.
2. Describe the type of volleyball program that your school offers.
3. Briefly describe the organization of the governing body for volleyball in the United States.
4. List five organizations that sponsor teams in USVBA open competition.

WHERE TO PLAY

5. State the date and site of one college or USVBA-sanctioned tournament or match in your region.
6. Explain how teams qualify for the USVBA National Volleyball tournament.

8

Further Study Materials

CONCEPT: Although "power" volleyball is seemingly a new sport on the highly competitive level, there is helpful material available on the advanced techniques of individual skills and team strategy.

BOOKS AND MAGAZINES

1. *Official Rules and Reference Guide.* Marvin D. Veronee, editor. United States Volleyball Association. $2.00 USVBA Printer, P.O. Box 109, Berne, Ind. 46711. Presents complete summary of past season, rules for coming season. Many informational and interesting articles.
2. *Volleyball Technical Journal for Coaches.* Lorne Sawula, editor. Canadian Volleyball Publications. Published Quarterly. $15. 78 Tedford Drive, Scarboro, Ontario, Canada MIR 1M4.
3. *Volleyball Guide.* Washington, D.C.: American Association for Health, Physical Education and Recreation, Division for Girls and Women's Sports, $1.75. Published biennially July 1973–July 1975. 1201 16th Street N.W., Washington, D.C. 20036. The official DGWS rules, officiating standards and techniques, with accompanying articles on playing, coaching, and teaching volleyball provide up-to-date materials and visual aids for the novice as well as the expert volleyball player."
4. *Official Volleyball Rules for Girls and Women: June 1973–June 1975* (reprint). Division for Girls and Women's Sports, American Association for Health, Physical Education and Recreation. $.50. 1201 16th St. N.W., Washington, D.C. 20036.
5. *Volleyball Review.* Henry C. Murray, editor. Official publication United States Volleyball Association. Published bimonthly (Jan., Mar., May, July, Sept., and Oct., $2 annually. Murray and Assoc., P.O. Box 995, San Leandro, Ca. 94511.
6. *Winning Volleyball,* Allen E. Scates, 1975, Allyn and Bacon, Inc., 470 Atlantic Avenue, Boston, Massachusetts 02210, 265 pp., $9.95. A complete guide for the player and coach who want a comprehensive

FURTHER STUDY MATERIALS

insight into this exciting sport. Whether you are involved with elementary school, high school, college or open volleyball, you can use the same strategy and techniques that led UCLA teams to become national collegiate champions in '65, '67, '70, '71, '72, '74 and '75. Hundreds of sequence and action photos accompany the techniques to be learned. Step-by-step learning sequences and drills to help the beginner master the basics. Detailed sections on duration and intensity of practice sessions, selection of offense and defense, and game plans. Many useful charts including line-up forms, strategy charts, and individual and team error charts. Allen E. Scates is the head coach of volleyball at UCLA, the 1971 and 1972 head coach for the USA Pan American and USA Olympic Teams, and Physical Education Specialist for the Beverly Hills Unified School District.

MOTION PICTURES

1. *Volleyball.* Official volleyball films of NCAA-AAHPER. Produced by Ealing Corporation. Young All-American and Olympic players demonstrate technically flawless volleyball fundamentals in slow motion analysis and freeze frame at critical teaching points. Cartridged Super-8mm Motion Pictures. Authored by Allen Scates, the set sells for $149.70. Individual loops of the Serve, Forearm Pass, Overhead Set, Spike, Block, and The Dive and The Roll can be purchased for $24.95. Order from NCAA Films, P.O. Box 2726, Wichita, Kansas 67201.

2. *Women's Volleyball Films*

   Film 1. USA-USSR, World Cup '73
   Film 2. USA-Korea, World Cup '73
   Film 3. USSR-Korea, World Cup '73
   Film 4. Korea-Japan, World Cup '73

   Films are Black & White with sound. Average running time is 33 minutes. Rental Price: $25.00 per day. For further information contact: Schreiber & Company, P.O. Box 24614, Los Angeles, Calif. 90024. (213) 475-4645.

COACHING AIDS

1. Spike-It. $64.50, Excel Sport Products. P.O. Box 251, Montrose, Calif. 91020. (213) 790-3988. The Spike-It allows players to concentrate on correct techniques rather than worrying about the placement of the set. Now a coach can teach approach, take-off, armswing and hand contact without waiting for the refinement of setting skills.

2. Block-It. $72.50, Excel Sport Products, P.O. Box 251, Montrose, Calif. 91020. (213) 790-3988. This is a device that rebounds the ball at random speeds in random directions—an essential tool for team drills designed to back up the spiker. The Block-It can also be used to prepare spikers to hit around the block or over it.

Glossary

I. OFFENSIVE MANEUVERS

Offense: Serving, passing, setting or attacking

A. Serving

Cross Court Serve: A serve landing near the opponent's right sideline.

Line Serve: A straight ahead serve landing near the opponent's left sideline.

Overhand Serve: A serve performed with an overhand throwing action.

Overhand Floater Serve: The overhand floater serve, having no spin, moves in an erratic path as it approaches the receiver. The ball is hit with only a momentary point of contact with very little follow-through.

Overhand Spin Serve: The ball is contacted on the lower midsection in the center; the heel of the server's hand first contacts the ball, and then the wrist snap rolls his hand over the ball, imparting topspin.

Roundhouse Serve: The arm moves in a windmill action, and the ball is contacted directly over the hitting shoulder.

Sky Ball Serve: This is an underhand serve that is hit so high it looks like it is falling straight down. It is used in large arenas or outdoor courts.

Underhand Serve: A serve performed with an underarm striking action. The ball is usually contacted with the heel of the hand.

B. Passing

Pass: The reception of the serve or first contact of the ball. It is an attempt to control the movement of the ball to another player. A pass of a hard spiked ball is called a dig.

Bump Pass: See Forearm Pass

Elbow Snap Pass: Starting with the elbows in a bent position and then extending them to a locked position just prior to contacting the ball.

Elbow Lock Pass: Arms remain locked before and during contact. Movement of the arms is directed in an arc from the shoulders.

Overhand Pass: Usually a pass executed with two hands in the same direction the passer is facing.

Forearm Pass: A ball played off the forearms in an underhand manner. It is the best way to pass a serve to the setter. It is also used to dig spikes and play any ball dropping close to the floor.

One-Arm Pass: See One-Arm Dig (II B Digging)

C. Setting

Set: A pass that places the ball in position for a player to spike.

Setter: The player who sets the ball to the spiker.

Back Set: A set made over the head, behind the setter, usually executed with two hands.

One Set: An extremely low vertical set delivered from 1 to 2 feet above the net. The spiker contacts the ball while the set is rising.

Slow One Set: A low vertical set that travels about 2 feet above the net. The spiker attacks the ball after it reaches its peak.

Two-Set: This set usually travels from 3-4 feet above the net. It does not require the same split second timing as the one set and can be mastered by any good spiker.

Three-Set: This play-set is delivered low and fast to the middle spiker about 10 feet from the left sideline. It was designed to beat a slow middle blocker.

Slow Three-Set: This play-set is lobbed 10 feet from the left sideline for the left attacker. It is most effective when the middle attacker can "freeze" the middle blocker with the threat of a quick hit.

Four Set: This set is placed about a foot from the sideline, at a height of 1 to 2 feet above the net. This play is very difficult for the middle blocker to cover when the ball travels a distance of 15-20 feet from the setter to the spiker.

Five-Set: A back lob to the setter on the right sideline is called a 5 set. It is low enough to create a one on one situation for the off hand spiker.

Regular Set: A ball that is delivered in a high arc that should drop about 2 ft. from the net, at either corner of the net.

GLOSSARY

Shoot Set: See Four Set.

Lateral Set: A set made to either side of the setter with two hands.

Normal Set: See regular set

One Hand Set: Many setters jump set passes that are going to travel over the net by intercepting the ball with the fingertips of one hand. This works particularly well for the one set to a quick middle attacker.

Punch Set: When the ball is going to be passed over the net and it is impossible to set the ball with two hands the backcourt setter may elect to punch set the ball with the knuckles rather than risk the chance of throwing the ball by contacting it with the fingertips.

Jump Set: The player setting the ball jumps to confuse the block or to place himself in a better position to save a long pass that will drop over or hit the net.

D. **Attacking**

Attacking: Hitting the ball into the opponent's court.

Cross Court Spike: A spike which is directed diagonally to the longest part of the court.

Dink: Usually a one hand hit in which the tips of the fingers are used to hit the ball to an area of the opponent's court.

Deep Dink: A dink that lands in the opponent's back court.

Follow-through: The attacker can reach over the net or follow through if he contacts the ball on his side first.

Line Spike: A spike directed down the side line closest to the spiker.

Off-hand Side: The side of the court on which the ball would have to cross in front of the spiker's body before contacting it with his predominant hand. For example, the right front corner would be the off-hand side for a right-handed spiker.

Off-Speed Shot: A ball that rapidly loses momentum due to a reduced speed of the striking arm just prior to contact. The off-speed shot is most effective when used infrequently and directed towards a definite weakness in the defense. The ball can be contacted by the hand or fingers for this shot.

On-Hand Side: The side of the court on which the spiker would contact the ball with his predominant hand before it would cross in front of his body. For example, the left front corner would be the on-hand side for a right-handed spiker.

Pre-Jump Takeoff: The spiker hops on his power foot to land simultaneously with both heels parallel; next he shifts his weight to the balls of the feet and bends his legs, then forceably contracts his legs, thereby forcing himself to leave the floor.

Round House Spike: A spike which is hit with a windmill action of the arm. The ball is usually contacted directly over the hitting shoulder with the body prependicular to the net.

Spike: A ball hit forceably with one hand. Backcourt players cannot spike the ball unless they take off from behind the ten foot striking line.

Spiker: A player who performs a spike, dink or off speed shot.

Step-Close Takeoff: The spiker takes a long last step by jumping forward, contacting the floor with the heel of one foot and then with the heel of the other foot; the weight then rolls from both heels to the toes as he takes off.

Tip: See Dink

Wipe-Off Spike: Refers to a conscious effort to spike the ball laterally off the block into the out of bounds area.

II. DEFENSIVE MANEUVERS

Defense: Blocking and digging.

A. Blocking

Block: A play by one or more players who attempt to intercept the ball over or near the net. Blocking is permitted by any or all of the players in the front line.

Attack Block: The attack block is an attempt to intercept the ball before it crosses the net.

Double Block: Two players are blocking at the net.

Down Block: Blockers drop their arms when they judge that the ball will not be hit by the spiker at a downward angle.

Key: A term used to describe close observation of an opposing player's habits or actions in order to gain a clue to his next move. For example, many blockers watch or "key" on the setter to see if he arches his back prior to contacting the ball. This action usually indicates a back set.

Key On the One Play: The middle blocker must jump with the middle attacker to stop the quick one set.

One-Hand Block: A technique used when the blocker is out of position. This maneuver gives the blocker greater lateral coverage above the net.

One On One Block: Used when the middle blocker cannot reach his assignment.

Single Block: One player is blocking at the net.

Soft Block: The forearms are held parallel to the net, hands held either tilted back or parallel to the net.

Triple Block: Three players are blocking at the net.

Turning the Ball In: A technique used by the end blocker to prevent the spike from hitting his hand and going out of bounds. He reaches over the net with his outside hand between the boundary line and the ball.

B. Digging

Dig: A pass of a spiked ball while standing, diving, rolling or jumping.

High Dig: Arms are held parallel to the floor when the flight of the ball permits, to enable the dig to travel high in the air on the digger's side of the net.

Backhand Dig: Hitting the ball with the back of the hand. During the dive this technique allows the player to keep his palms close to the floor in anticipation of a quick landing.

Cushion the Ball: Digging the ball with a backward movement of the arms or body.

Dive: An attempt to recover a ball by going to a prone position on the court.

One-Arm Dig: This technique is used when the ball cannot be contacted using the forearm pass. The ball can be effectively contacted anywhere from the knuckles of the closed fist to the elbow joint.

Roll: A lateral movement that allows the players to go to the floor without injury and return him quickly to his feet. Ideally the ball is contacted just before the thigh and buttocks hit the floor.

III. TEAM DEFENSE

Area Block: Blocking a designated area of the net. Frequently used when good diggers are in the back court.

Blue Defense: See Off Blocker Defense

Free Ball: When the defense sees that the offense will hit the ball over the net with an upward flight or weak spike, it should call, "Free!" and assume a normal serve reception pattern.

False Weakness: This is a play used to lure the opposition into spiking to an area that they think is weak. For example, a blocker may leave the area above the net open for a crosscourt shot and then quickly swing his arms to the middle of the net just prior to the spiker contacting the ball.

Middle Back Defense: A defensive formation that utilizes the middle back player to recover deep spikes.

Middle In Defense: A defensive formation that utilizes the middle back player to recover short dink shots.

Off Blocker Defense: A defensive formation that utilizes the off blocker to recover short dink shots.

Red Defense: See Middle In Defense

White Defense: See Middle Back Defense

Zone Block: See Area Block

IV. TEAM OFFENSE

Combinations: A play that involves two attackers penetrating into a single blocker's zone of the net.

1. *Double Quick:* The middle attacker approaches for a one set and the off-hand attacker approaches for a back one set. This play usually isolates the middle blocker who must defend against two attackers.

2. *Right Cross:* The middle attacker approaches for a one set and the right attacker crosses behind him for a two set. The setter watches the middle blocker and sets to the open spiker.

3. *Tandem:* The middle attacker approaches for a one set and the left attacker follows right behind him for a two set. The setter watches the middle blocker; if the middle blocker jumps with the first attacker, the setter delivers a two set to the second man.

Four-Man Reception: Four-man receiving formations are very efficient if four superior passers are receiving the serve. The advantage of this system is that the player approaching for the one-set has a better approach because he starts at the net and has little serve recciving responsibility.

Five-One Offense: This offense uses 5 hitters and one setter. Consequently 50% of the rotations the offense runs with 3 hitters and 50% of the rotations it runs with 2 hitters at the net. One player sets all the good passes.

Multiple Offense: A two or three hitter system that utilizes play sets.

One-On-One Situation: This refers to one attacker spiking against one blocker. Most offenses run their patterns with one-on-one situations as their goal.

Percentage Play: Certain sets can be hit with a better spiking percentage in certain situations. For example, when the ball

GLOSSARY

is passed about 15 feet from the net, the best percentage set is a regular set. The attacker would have a poor spiking average if the setter delivered a quick set on a bad pass.

Play Sets: These are sets used to create favorable attack conditions. Plays are called by the setter or the attacker to avoid the block. Plays set vary greatly in height and distance from the setter to the attacker.

Six-Two Offense: This is an offense that uses three hitters at the net and a back row setter. Four players are spikers and two are setter-spikers.

Technique Player: The technique player is primarily a spiker who sets the ball only when he is in the right back position.

Three-Hitter Attack: The offense used when a backcourt setter is utilized.

Two-Hitter Attack: The offense used when one of the front court players is a setter.

V. MISCELLANEOUS

Antenna: A pole extending vertically from the bottom of the net to a height of 2-1/2 to 3-1/2 feet above the net at the sideline.

Contacted Ball: A contacted ball is one that touches or is touched by any part of a player's body or clothing.

Foul: A failure to play the ball properly as permitted under the rules.

Gather: The act of squatting just prior to jumping.

Netting: Touching the net while the ball is in play. This act terminates play when seen by the referee or umpire. In doubles, the player calls his own nets.

Out of Bounds: The ball is out of bounds when it touches any surface or object or ground outside the court, or touches the net outside the markers on the sides of the net, or touches a net antenna, or passes over the net not entirely within the net antennas.

Scoring: A team can only score points when they are serving.

Screw Under: A technique used by a player to put himself in a more favorable position to play the ball by taking a long step with his lead leg and squatting. His trailing leg is extending as he pivots toward the ball. This technique is used to pass, dig or set the ball.

Seam: The area directly between two serve receivers or diggers.

Short Court: The official doubles court is 30 feet by 50 feet. This rule is largely ignored as doubles players throughout the country continue to use the 30 feet by 60 foot court.

Side Out: When the serving team fails to score a point the ball is given to their opponents and exchange of service is called a side-out.

Specialist: Functional designation by position or ability. For example a player who is substituted across the back row to dig is a "back court specialist."

Thrown Ball: The ball must be clearly hit. When, in the opinion of the proper official, the ball visibly comes to rest at contact, the player shall have committed a foul.

Transition: Changing from offense to defense or vice versa.